# Guinea PIG for BREAKFAST

A rich tapestry of tragedy,
hope and love in Ecuador

ANDREA GARDINER

Grosvenor House
Publishing Limited

This book is published by
Grosvenor House Publishing Ltd
28-30 High Street, Guildford, Surrey, GU1 3EL.
www.grosvenorhousepublishing.co.uk

A CIP record for this book
is available from the British Library

Some of the names in this book have been
changed to protect some individuals' identity

ISBN 978-1-78148-580-4

For my girls Tamara Rachel and Emily Megan, the most precious gifts from God.

# Contents

# CONTENTS

# Prologue

I opened my bleary eyes in confusion as Tamara rushed into our bedroom waving a cooked, whole guinea-pig she had extracted from the fridge. "Want meat, want meat Mummy" she cried. I am not at my best at six o clock in the morning, and being woken in such a manner did not help matters. "Surely you can't want guinea-pig for breakfast," I moaned into my pillow.

Living in Ecuador was never dull, that was for sure. Every day brought new surprises and challenges. My children were more used to eating green bananas and chicken feet soup than a good old cheese sandwich, or baked beans on toast. They rode their great-granny's horses bareback, and swam in the village river. They sucked oranges fresh from the trees in the garden, and watermelons grown on our farm. They wondered why I freaked out if they wanted to get on a motorbike like the other children around them did, and did not run in long grass for fear of snakes.

Sometimes everything seemed so alien and weird to me; life seemed unsafe and very unpredictable. I felt like I had no control over what happened to my family. I wondered if I were being utterly irresponsible for bringing up my daughters in this environment.

Sometimes life seemed amazing. Sometimes we had the chance to change a life, to touch the untouchables, to be God's hands for precious children everyone else had forgotten.

When I visited Señora Clemencia who has a grotesque tumour obliterating and distorting half her face, my baby gladly went into her arms, too young to be bothered by a sight most people flinched at and turned away from. She smiled her beautiful smile up at Señora Clemencia, and gazed straight into her eyes, making Señora Clemencia feel special and loved. It was a moment made in heaven. It was a moment that made me glad I kept going through the tough times. It was a moment that made me sure it was not time to go home.

## CHAPTER ONE

# The Middle of the World

I sat bewildered and afraid in the small car negotiating its way through the turbulent streets of Quito. Angry citizens were flocking into the streets throwing stones and setting up road blocks with burning tyres. The Police were out in equal force spraying tear gas that caused panic as people dodged and ran, choking as the irritant gas stole their breath.

The then President of Ecuador, Lucio Gutierrez, was in the process of being kicked out. The people were angry with him and the corruption of his government. It was havoc; shouts, bangs and screams filled the air.

"This is not exactly the reception I imagined as I set off for my big adventure on the equator." I thought as we negotiated the riots. I wanted to be able to quietly get on and use my medical skills to help the poor. I had come to love the sick children and do all I could to make them better. I was not expecting my life to be in danger in the process. Martyr missionary stories were all very well, but I was not that brave. I was just an ordinary person who wanted to give something back. I wondered how those around me carried on as if nothing unusual was happening; until it struck me this might in fact be usual for Ecuador. A shiver went down my spine as I feared I had bitten off more than I could chew. I wished I understood the Spanish being gabbled around me, and what was really going on. I felt so disorientated and isolated. I really hoped to arrive in safety soon.

"Welcome to Ecuador!" exclaimed my hosts Carmen and Jorge with great warmth and affection as I finally arrived at my destination. "Don't be alarmed," they reassured me as they took in the shocked expression on my face, "Here Presidents rarely last longer than a year in office. Let's go up on the roof so we can see what is happening."

From the roof we had a perfect view of the airport. There, to my amazement, we witnessed the President fleeing the country in a helicopter as protestors invaded the runway and tried to stop him escaping. "What kind of a place is this?" I wondered to myself. "It is like something out of a movie, not real life. I have prepared so many years to come here, have longed to able to come back and be useful, but nothing could have prepared me for this. How am I ever going to be able to attend patients if the country is constantly in uproar? Maybe coming here is one big mistake."

I was surprised – and relieved - to see how quickly everything returned to normal. Maybe God did have work for me to do after all. The Vice-President, Alfredo Palacios, took power. He was a medical doctor, and putting their faith in him the doctors in the public sector, who had been on strike for the previous nine weeks in protest at not being paid, went back to work. I gladly settled into life in Quito, studying Spanish with a private tutor in the afternoons, and enjoying family life and watching fantastic Latin American soap operas on the television in the evenings. Gradually I began to relax and enjoy my gentle introduction to Ecuadorean culture.

Carmen cooked me wonderful Ecuadorian food typical of the mountain regions. She made warming soups with potato, cheese, corn on the cob and beans. One dish I really enjoyed was boiled broad beans and sweet corn served with cheese. We had beef and chicken and plenty of potatoes and bananas. She also used her liquidiser to whisk up amazing fruit juices and milkshakes from the abundance of fresh fruit grown in Ecuador.

She taught me that Ecuador has several climates; the cold mountains, the tropical rain forest and the hot, humid coastal plains. Each region has its own produce and traditional dishes. The mountain people grow potatoes, broccoli, carrots, apples, plums and beans, and enjoy cooking guinea-pig and pork. The coastal people grow manioc, bananas, and maize, and eat an abundance of fish and shellfish. The jungle people grow bananas and peanuts. They eat fish caught in their rivers, and hunt wild animals such as guatuso (an animal similar to a large rabbit), forest boar and sometimes monkey.

Jorge was a wonderful grandpa who had worked most of his life for the French Embassy. He had an ancient falling to bits Renault which amazingly he still managed to keep running most of the time. He was generous and helpful to a fault. He was very proud of his traditions and typical dishes.

When some American vegetarians came to visit he cooked them a special barbeque of succulent steaks and tasty chicken. He thought being vegetarian meant liking vegetables, and could not grasp that anyone would actually not eat any meat. His hospitality demanded he keep pressing it on them, and out of politeness they really had to give in and look like they were enjoying it.

He then regaled them with stories from his childhood, growing up in a small village in the mountains. He recounted how he used to slit the necks of bulls and drink the warm blood as it gushed out to make him manlier. I loved hearing his tales, he told them with such gusto and enthusiasm – but I have to confess I did not translate that story entirely accurately for the vegetarians.

I was taken aback when he arrived home with a guinea-pig one afternoon, bopped it on the head, and skinned it ready for barbequing. "You have to try this," he assured me, "it is the most delicious meat." I thought of the cute pets back home, and my stomach turned at the thought of eating one of the furry creatures. Jorge carried on oblivious, impaling the poor animal on a skewer and rotating it with great care over the burning coals. His mouth was watering. "How can I get out of this one?" I wondered to myself wildly, not seeing any avenue of escape.

Sure enough soon the guinea-pig was proclaimed perfectly cooked, with crispy skin and succulent juicy meat. I was served a leg. There was no way out. I was going to have to eat it. Screwing up my courage (and my eyes) I took a bite and chewed hurriedly. It was at least edible I had to admit to myself, although I did not think I would ever be able to munch it with the look of ecstasy that appeared on Jorge's face as he ate what was his favourite delicacy. Clearly serving as a doctor in Ecuador was going to involve many more challenges than simply clinical problems. My initiation into Ecuadorean culture did not seem so tame anymore.

Jorge and Carmen took me out and about and, being accustomed to hosting foreigners, taught me Ecuadorean manners. It felt strange to me to have to greet everyone I met with a handshake or a kiss on the cheek. It felt too familiar, an invasion of my personal space.

This was no place to be shy and reserved. I was expected to confidently speak out when I entered a room where people were eating to say "buen provecho" meaning "enjoy your meal". I could never slip away unnoticed from a gathering, but had to screw up my courage and make sure I went round each person present in turn to say goodbye, again with a kiss.

When addressing people who had a title it was polite to use it; for example calling medical doctors, dentists and lawyers "Doctor so and so" and science graduates "Engineer". I had to get used to people calling me "Doctorita" in an affectionate use of my title. They rarely used my name.

When in conversation regarding the height of some children I was taken aback by my companion's disapproval of my hand gestures. "You must not hold your hand horizontally to indicate the height of humans," she told me in shocked tones. "We only do that when we are talking about animals. For humans you must hold your hand vertically." I felt embarrassed and realised I still had a lot to learn. Forget being a qualified General Practitioner - I felt like I was back in school learning the basics in life over again.

My Spanish tutor, Rita, took me on outings to learn more of the Ecuadorian culture. We took a trip to the Middle of the World, a museum on the equator, where they had an exhibition of the different people groups of Ecuador, their dress and their instruments.

I found it fascinating to be introduced to the several distinct indigenous Indian groups in Ecuador; each with their own customs and languages. I loved learning about them. The indigenous people who live in the mountain regions have highly embroidered warm clothes, ponchos and hats and play the pan pipes. They make brightly coloured woollen bags and wall hangings which tourists love to buy. I stocked up on some to send home to my family.

Coastal and jungle people groups tend to wear minimal clothing due to the heat they live in, but paint their bodies with bold lines and play instruments such as xylophones and drums. They make string bags and hammocks.

There are African groups too, descendents of people who were brought to the country during the time of the slave trade. They regale their audiences with merengue dancing as they show off their pulsating sense of rhythm.

In the streets of Quito I would see Quichua Indians in their traditional shawls, long skirts and hats, mixing with the Mestizo population in their western style of dress as they went about their business, creating an intriguing tapestry of the traditional and the modern.

A cable car opened while I was in Quito, climbing up to fourteen thousand feet on the side of Pichincha Volcano. The views from the top were breathtaking on a clear morning. You could see the circle of crystalline snow topped volcanoes surrounding the city, and the city itself contained in the valley below. Looking down from above the houses, the airport and the cars below all seemed like toys. You could not see the hustle and bustle of business men and women rushing to work, students attending their schools and universities, and the crush of people on the trams and buses.

Getting about the city on the ground was a different story. There were so many people squeezed into such a small space. I hated people constantly touching me as I went about my daily affairs. People bumped into me in the street as they squeezed through gaps that did not exist. The buses were one big crush of humanity, and I had to screw up my courage to step on each day and endure another half an hour of being up close and personal with perfect strangers.

I became very tired of it, especially as the less scrupulous used these circumstances as a chance to pick pockets and bags. I was almost home when some men pressed up against me as I tried to get off the bus. I was so concerned about holding on to my bag that I forgot to watch my jeans front pocket where I had my purse. I finally managed to squeeze myself off the bus and standing alone on the pavement breathed a sigh of relief - until I realised my purse had gone, along with my bank card that I needed to be able to access my money in the U.K. Tears rose unbidden to my eyes as my heart sank. "How dare they steal from me," I raged, "I am just minding my own business, trying to learn Spanish so that I can help the people here, and this is the payment I receive. Sometimes I wonder why I put myself through all this." Images of the tranquil Scottish islands from whence I had come sprang unbidden to my mind. Life there had been so safe and secure. I trudged wearily back to the house somewhat dispirited.

Jorge took me to the police station to report the loss. It was a dingy underground office full of policemen sitting at type-writers. When it was my turn I had to describe the circumstances of the theft to an officer while he clumsily bashed away at his keyboard typing up a report of the incident. This document was then photocopied, stamped and given to me. "This is the most ridiculous procedure ever," I complained to Jorge on the way home in his falling-to-bits car. "This document can only serve for any possible insurance claim. They make no attempt whatsoever to stop such crimes being perpetrated again in the future, do they? The thieves get off scot free. I feel so powerless. I can see there can be no justice here."

The sun blazed during the day and late afternoon the rains would come. I always tried to be home by then, because the heavens literally opened and bucketed down the rain.

If I was out in it I was soaked in seconds. Thunder and lightening were common as well. The power cables sparked throughout the storms in an alarming manner and power cuts were frequent. The nights when the power went off early, I used to snuggle up in bed under the heavy woollen blankets to keep warm, as once the sun went down the temperature dropped dramatically, and the houses did not have any heating.

From time to time the whole house shook as an earth tremor hit. Being in a volcanic region these were common and no one else paid much attention to everything shuddering and vibrating for a few seconds. Only I appeared to be afraid of them and I wondered how long it would take me to consider them a normal part of life, for me to feel at home in this adopted country of mine. I had yearned to come here for so long; felt inexplicably drawn to the people who lived here, somehow incapable of ignoring their need for help. I was intending to stay for the long haul. I wanted to get settled in as soon as possible.

To be able to practice as a doctor in Ecuador I first had to revalidate my medical degree. I had brought with me all the required documents duly translated and notarised to present to an Ecuadorian medical school for them to agree that I had completed an equivalent degree to their own.

It was to be an education in how grindingly slowly bureaucracy functioned in Ecuador. Each week I spoke to Señora Margarita, secretary at the University, to ask how the revalidation of my degree was advancing.

"Good Morning Doctor," she cheerily greeted me, "Yes, yes, we will have some news for you next week."

"But you said the same thing last week." I pointed out in frustration.

"The committee is reviewing your case. Come back again next week," was the standard reply.

At first I naively believed her polite assurances, and then as time went on and no progress was made I became increasingly frustrated and annoyed at the utter lack of efficiency.

"You would have thought that having a medical degree from Edinburgh University, Scotland recognised as valid in Ecuador would be a matter of course." I muttered to myself. "I even fondly supposed that Ecuadoreans might welcome the arrival of my expertise to help some of their population and facilitate the process. But they are so utterly inefficient and slow! I wonder if I am ever going to receive the papers I need. But I know others have managed it, so it must be possible. I am just going to have to be patient and keep insisting. Maybe it will be character building – God must want to teach me patience."

Suddenly as I meandered back to the house, returning from an unproductive visit to the University, I was startled by a man appearing out of nowhere behind me. He put his arms around me and grabbed my breasts, then ran off as suddenly as he had arrived. I did not even get a look at him. I was first paralysed by shock, then started to run as fast as I could to the house. I was extremely relieved to get myself inside the big metal gates that guarded the entrance. Shaken, I made my way inside and calmed down over a cup of camomile tea with the ever reassuring and motherly Carmen.

"Doctorita don't cry," she consoled me, "No harm came to you. God was protecting you."

"Yes, yes, I am fine, just a bit shocked by the experience." I claimed, trying to put a brave face on it and not wanting to make a scene. Inside I was jelly, shaken by my vulnerability.

I escaped to the quiet of my room and could not stop thinking about how I might have felt if the man had attacked me. Would I still want to pursue my dream of helping the poor in Ecuador? How high a price was I willing to pay for being here? A shiver of fear ran down my spine as I imagined what could have happened that evening. But I was determined not to give in to that fear. "One perverse man is not going to sway me from my hopes and plans." I told myself sternly. "Surely God would not bring me this far, through so much preparation, and plant this dream in my heart only to have something awful happen to me as soon as I arrive. I will not be afraid to continue this journey. I will trust in God to protect me. But I think that I am ready to leave the big city and head to my final destination. I have had enough of Quito."

So it was that two months after my arrival in the country, having completed my language study, I found myself on the bus heading to Santo Domingo, as yet still without permission to work as a doctor.

Despite all the trials and frustrations I was filled with a great sense of excitement and anticipation. Finally I would be able to settle into the village I had wanted to come to work in for so many years.

I remembered my first visit as a green eighteen year old on a summer team, when I had seen poverty in person for the first time; meeting shoeless children in rags, and visiting families living in ramshackle homes cobbled together with plastic and bamboo had left an indelible impression. Seeing it in person was so different to just seeing images on the television.

I remembered little Juan whose finger had had to be amputated because no one had kept his wound clean, and it had tragically developed gangrene. Such unnecessary suffering had etched itself in my conscience. I had put my photo of his cute little face up in my room wherever I had travelled, his shy smile melting my heart each time I caught a glimpse of it. I could not ignore his plight.

I pictured the teenage couple who had offered me their baby, willing to make the sacrifice of giving up their child because they thought I could give him a better life than they could. The encounter had left me churning with emotions in the pit of my stomach as I wondered what terrible circumstances had driven them to such a desperate decision. As I had rocked the beautiful baby girl in my arms I had whispered that I would return. I would return to help these precious children that Jesus longed to bless.

I thought of the anaemic children with their swollen bellies full of worms that had shown such affection to the white visitors that summer as we had played with them in the slum. They had showered me with hugs and kisses. They had become my friends. No longer was poverty something I watched detached on the television. It was something awful that was causing haunted expressions and eyes lacking in hope in tiny children that I now knew and cared about. I had suddenly realised how utterly blessed I was; a loving family, a first class education, and the knowledge that Jesus loved me. I had never wanted for anything. And now I felt compelled to do something for those who did not enjoy those blessings. I could not stay comfortably in Scotland while children were dying and I had the means to help them. I had pursued medical training for ten years after that first visit to Ecuador, with the goal of having sufficient experience to be able to return and be useful. The voices of the children calling me to go back and help them had never quietened in all that time. Along the way I had half hoped maybe a handsome young man might appear wanting to accompany me to the middle of the world. But such men seemed to be in small supply. Young, free, single and undeterred, at last I was realising my dream.

I was excited and itching to get started.

## CHAPTER TWO

# City of Red Indians

Santo Domingo de los Colorados, named for its indigenous Indians who paint their hair red, was a far cry from the relative sophistication of Quito. The city had grown rapidly, from a handful of families to four hundred thousand inhabitants in the short space of time of forty years. The city was a sprawling chaos, lacking drinking water, an adequate sewage system and covered by a messy intertwining of electricity cables resembling a plate of spaghetti. Organisation was unheard of. The Mayor had a beautiful hotel with a swimming pool and patio lined with plaques thanking him for his public works, yet the streets remained un-surfaced: thick mud in the rainy season and dust bowls in the dry season.

As I wandered through the centre of town throngs of people crowded the streets going about their business and bumping and jostling me in the process. Cries of, "Oranges for sale, ten for a dollar!" filled the air. The strident insistent hooting of the cars and buses assaulted my ears and the smell of exhaust fumes mixed with the stench of rotting vegetables filled my nostrils. The people who greeted me were young, open and laid-back.

They dressed informally, laughed with abandon, cried with passion and gave hospitality with great generosity.

I found the constant heat and extreme humidity exhausting at first. I was constantly bathed in a shiny, sticky sweat from morning to evening. I never felt clean. Nothing lasted very long in this climate. Wood rotted and was invaded by wood worm. I was dismayed to find my towels and clothing became filled with mildew and quickly developed holes. Keeping things in an enclosed space such as a drawer was a recipe for mould and cockroaches.

I lived in a village just outside the town, in an orphanage for AIDS victims called Orphaids. It was a welcome escape from the noisy, dirty city. Here in the countryside there was an astonishing variety of exotic brightly coloured flowers, in what resembled an eternal spring. The emerald green landscape was covered with banana plantations, maize and manioc. I loved hearing the birds singing as I woke in the morning and watching the glittering humming birds darting between the flowers in the garden. I felt privileged and happy to be able to live in such a beautiful corner of the world. Being back in the countryside revived my flagging spirits.

The wild life tried to encroach on the house on a regular basis. The worst was the sensation of the tickly feet of huge cockroaches running over me in bed at night making me scream in fright. There were ants of all shapes and sizes, which seemed just to know when there was a speck of sweetness left lying around, and which managed to get into the sugar tub, cereal packets and even loaves of bread. I soon resigned myself to eating them on occasion. The occasional bat found its way into the house, and had to be coaxed, or forced out by a handy orphan wielding a bat, and mice came in and nibbled holes in belongings from time to time. One morning I was surprised to see an ornamental frog sitting by the fireplace, which I did not remember being there before, until I realised of course it was not an ornament, but alive, and hastily found a tub to trap it in so that I could restore it to the great outdoors. A cheeky orphan looking on chuckled as I jumped when the frog leapt away. "This is no place to be squeamish," I told myself sternly. "You have come here to make yourself useful. You should expect some discomforts."

There was a plague of millipedes when I arrived. They were small and black and curled up into a spiral if you touched them. Underfoot they were crunchy, and there were so many I could not avoid walking on them as I went along the road. There were millions. Armies of them marched in formation to their unknown destination. I took them on as a challenge to my ingenuity. At night I stuffed newspaper around the front door to stop them coming in, and sprayed it with insecticide to kill those that still managed to find an entrance. In the mornings I had hundreds lying dead by the door waiting to be swept up and disposed of. They got into everything; food, clothes, plates, saucepans, beds and even ears. I was very thankful when they all disappeared as suddenly as they had appeared.

Before I could start work I had to learn how to do the daily chores. To go shopping I had to get myself into town on the "ranchera", an open sided bus that I had to climb up on to and then squeeze myself into non-existent spaces on the hard benches that formed the seating. The bus bumped along the unmade roads into town, covering us all with clouds of dust in the dry season and spattering us with rain in the wet season. Inexpert in riding the beast, I often fell off the thing as I arrived back home, clutching my shopping bags desperately. I covered myself in bruises in my haste to disembark before the impatient driver went on his way again. It made me think twice before venturing into town.

Eventually, fed up of being jolted around on the ranchera, I decided to treat myself to a taxi ride home. As I came out of the internet café a fellow client pointed out his taxi and offered me a ride. I explained where I wanted to go, negotiated the price, and off we went - but I soon realised he was not going the normal route home. When I pointed this out to him, thinking he had made a simple mistake, he laughed and said he wanted to take me to a swimming pool, before taking me to my house.

"But sir," I protested in alarm, "I do not want to go to a swimming pool. I asked you to take me home."

The taxi man took no notice, "No, no, señorita" he chuckled, "It is a lovely swimming pool. You will enjoy it and we will be able to get to know each other."

I was now terrified, not knowing the streets we were driving along, and wanting to get out of the car. "What on earth is this man going to do?" I asked myself in a panic. "I don't want to become further acquainted with him. How dare he just take me off like this! Or is he going to take me somewhere to attack me? What do I do now? Maybe I should try and jump out of the car now. I should have just taken the ranchera home." Just then we arrived at the swimming pool. He turned to invite me in for a swim, and appeared sincerely astonished that I was now in tears.

"Why are you crying Señorita?" He jovially exclaimed, "I am only being your friend and showing you where you can have fun in Santo Domingo."

I hastily exited the taxi without futile further comment, and hailed a different one, which did take me directly home. I fumed to myself, "How dare he just take me against my will and scare me like that! I need to protect myself better against these Latin men who seem to think they can do as they please with women. I am not going to survive here very long otherwise. I've heard that missionaries have been raped here. I don't want that to happen to me; it doesn't even bear thinking about. I just want to be able to get on with doctoring people in peace."

Finally back in the safety of Orphaids I bumped into Victor, a five year old orphan with severe cerebral palsy. "Hello Victor." I greeted him, and he rewarded me with his delightful grin that lit up his whole face. Needing a distraction from the fright I had suffered I stopped to chat to Janet, his carer.

"What is Victor's story?" I asked her.

"Victor was born in a state hospital to a mother who was terminally ill with AIDS, Tuberculosis and syphilis.

She passed all three diseases on to her wee baby, and then abandoned him."

"How did he come to the orphanage?" I asked.

"The social worker knew of us, and asked us to take him. He was very sick and no other orphanage would have him. He almost died many times, but through the dedicated nursing of his house parents he pulled through."

"It must have been very difficult to care for him." I commented.

"He used to cry all night long." Janet agreed. "It was very draining looking after him, but the people here grew to love him and did everything possible to care for him. Gradually he became stronger, as you can see."

"You are doing a great job," I commended Janet as I gazed at Victor, such a broken little boy, unable to speak or walk, needing to be fed and have his nappy changed. It was a miracle he had survived, I reflected. Yet here he was smiling, content and well cared for. He was being shown the love of God each and every day. "It is to make this kind of a difference in people's lives that I have come," I reminded myself. "This is why I am willing to put up with cockroaches, bureaucracy and dangers. I will not be discouraged."

I had not come to find a man. I was determined to enjoy the freedom of being single, and keep focussed on becoming established as a doctor and getting to work. I felt like I stood out like a beacon in Santo Domingo, with my light hair and green eyes, receiving wolf whistles as I walked down the street. I was uncomfortable being the object of so much unwanted male attention and did my best to feign being oblivious to it. "The men here are so obnoxious," I thought, "There is no way I am going to fall for one of them."

Some would not be ignored, such as the local village policeman, who asked me to marry him despite the fact others told me he had a wife and four children at home. A neighbour, known as Mr Boots because he was always wearing his wellies, also asked for my hand in marriage, his enormous tummy protruding from his tatty T-shirt. "You will never have to wash the dishes," he promised me earnestly as he forcibly grasped and kissed my hand, "Just bear my children." I just laughed these ridiculous offers off out of hand and refused to be distracted from my goals.

When I was alone at night, however, I did wonder if there was any possibility of a nice British man coming along, who shared my passion to serve the poor. I wanted to stay here for a long time, to have the chance to make a real difference, but in my heart of hearts I was not at all sure I was willing to give up the opportunity to have a family of my own in the process. It was a desire I had to put in God's hands over and over again.

Settling in to life in the village was harder than I had thought it would be. Still learning to understand the Spanish gabbled around me at a great rate, I felt like there was a barrier between me and the locals, as I struggled to decipher their meaning at times. I fell into bed at night exhausted with the effort required to simply communicate.

There was so much I took for granted at home that I had to learn over again in Ecuador. I could no longer rely on piped gas, but had to buy cylinders. Sometimes there was a shortage and it meant queuing up an entire day to be able to obtain one. I could no longer rely on there being electricity all the time. There were frequent power cuts in the dry season, as the country's power supply was hydroelectric. I learned to have candles at the ready at night time, and always to unplug everything that was not in use in case a power surge or lightening damaged them. I could no longer pay with my debit card, but had to learn to survive in a cash society. Everything from an apple to a house had to be paid for in cash. Similarly all bills had to be paid in person. Gone were the days of direct debits covering the month's expenses. Now I had to queue up in offices and banks in town to pay the electricity bill, taxes and mobile phone charges. These chores had become arduous.

Every week I made a 'phone call to Margarita, the friendly secretary at the University in Quito. "Good day Señora Margarita," I began, "It is Doctora Andrea from Santo Domingo calling to see what news there is on the revalidation of my medical degree."

"Good day Doctorita. What a pleasure to hear from you. Yes the committee is considering your case and we will have news for you soon."

"But when will that be? Is there some problem with my papers?"

"The committee has a meeting on Thursday next week. I should have news for you after that."

"Very well, I shall 'phone you again next week then."

"Yes, yes Doctorita, it is always a pleasure to hear from you. Take care."

"Good bye." I hung up the telephone more frustrated than ever. "How long are they going to take over this?" I wondered, tearing my hair out. "I could be old and grey by the time I have permission to set to work at this rate. What can I do to chivvy them up?" My prayers to become a registered doctor in Ecuador seemed to be falling on deaf ears.

As I settled into life in the village word soon got around that a doctor had arrived, and although I could not officially start work as a doctor yet people soon started arriving at the house asking for help. Being able to start assisting the people gave me the inspiration I needed to persevere in overcoming the frustrations of life.

Doña Maura came to see me with her teenage son. "Doctor," she cried with tears in her eyes, "my son is very, very ill. He has had a sore throat for three days now, and can hardly bear the pain. I am frightened he might die, so I took him to a doctor and he prescribed these injections, but they are going to cost one hundred dollars. I am poor and I will have to sell my pig to be able to buy them. Can you help me?"

I read the prescription and was distraught to see that he had been prescribed strong antibiotics to be injected into a vein at home that could, when given in high doses, cause deafness. I checked his throat then giving him some ibuprofen (which had cost me a few cents) told them, "Take one of these tablets three times a day. These will take away the pain and you will be better in no time."

And indeed he was. "Doctorita," Doña Maura called out to me the next day as I passed by her house, "My son is already so much better! He went to school today. They are powerful tablets." I felt on top of the world.

I wondered what would cause a doctor to prescribe in such an extravagant and, in my opinion, dangerous manner.

Mary, a British lady who had retired to the village with her husband as volunteers, helped me think things through. Many doctors in Ecuador were private. They made money from consultation fees and also from the medicines they sold. This naturally gave rise to the temptation to prescribe expensive treatments, even when there were more economic alternatives available.

Mary explained, "Patients in Ecuador love injections. They believe they work better than tablets. Our farm workers are always asking for us to buy them injections for illnesses such as the common cold. Ignorance makes people very afraid of illness, and often they think simple problems are fatal. It makes them very vulnerable to those who would exploit them."

I decided a good way to find out more about these local beliefs and to start to combat this ignorance would be to teach a group of women from the village to be health promoters. It would be a good use of my time until my paperwork came through.

Mary helped me get together those ladies who were already used by the community to treat their wounds, give them their injections and advise them on their health problems. They were an enthusiastic bunch, who loved what they did and were excited at the chance to learn more. As we discussed the basics of hygiene and nutrition, common ailments and their treatments, first aid and health promotion, I learnt as much from them about local ideas and practices, as they did from me about modern medicine. We had great fun role-playing and debating, sharing stories and experiences, practicing bandaging and giving injections. "This is great," I thought to myself after the first few classes, "I am learning so much and I think they are too. They are much more open to new ideas than I thought they might be."

Monserrat shared how people wanted their medicine given as an injection or even better as a drip into a vein. I explained that often tablets were just as effective, and avoided the risks of an injection. Hortencia talked about neighbours asking her to give them intravenous vitamin drips in their homes, to give them more strength or to help them gain weight. Nora explained local remedies for common problems, such as putting urine in ears for fungal infections, and dropping breast milk into eyes for conjunctivitis.

They acted out being their husbands drunk by the village shop, smoking cigarettes, when we talked about risk factors for heart disease, and they explained the importance of the extended family in caring for sick relatives and protecting the vulnerable from abuse. They complained many men were "macho" and irresponsible towards their families, and I soon had an example of this arrive on my doorstep.

It was early in the morning and I was still asleep when there was a knock at the door, and Monserrat called for me urgently, "Doctorita there is a woman here about to give birth." I fervently hoped this was some sort of joke as I stumbled to the door in my pyjamas bleary eyed, only to find to my horror a young woman groaning with labour pains.

"Come in, come in" I repeated as I ushered them in the door. The young woman sank on to the tiled floor exhausted and as I examined her I could see the baby's head. "Quick Monserrat" I cried, "bring me my bag please." I hurriedly pulled on a pair of gloves as the baby slithered out into the world, and hunted wildly for something sterile to tie and cut the cord with. Monserrat was the picture of composure as she wrapped the baby boy in a towel and handed him to his Mum to suckle, while I was sweating and trying to remember how to deliver the placenta.

Once order was restored, and Rocio was sleeping on the sofa exhausted, Monserrat told me the rest of the story as she rocked the sweet baby in her arms.

"Rocio is the mother of three children, and her husband abandoned her a few weeks ago. He left her alone in a remote shack with their toddlers, with no money to be able to get to the hospital when her time came. When she went into labour this morning she had to walk two miles to get to my house, and by then she was so close to giving birth I thought it best to bring her to you instead of trying to make it to the hospital in town."

Rocio's brother later came to collect her from my house, and took her and her children to live with him. I continued my conversation with Monserrat.

"Does this kind of thing happen often?" I asked, desperately hoping the answer was going to be "no". I did not fancy delivering babies on my floor too regularly.

"Men here are not responsible, they are macho." She replied firmly. "He probably has another woman somewhere else, or got tired of working to provide for his family. There are many single mothers who struggle to survive. Usually their parents help them, or the children would go hungry. It is how life is."

"But why do the women not stand up for themselves?" I exclaimed, impacted by this calm acceptance of the status quo.

"How can we?" Monserrat replied. "Most women have had no education to speak of. We cannot find work. We have no resources with which to change our circumstances. They have no choice but to accept what destiny brings us. We have to be careful not to upset our husbands or they might hit us. We cannot leave because we need the men to be able to pay for our children's education."

I was shocked into silence. I could not imagine how it must feel to be so impotent, utterly at the mercy of others. I was outraged at these abuses on my doorstep and I began to ponder how I could make a difference to these women.

At first I wanted to help everyone I met. The stories people came to me with tugged at my heart strings. I was full of enthusiasm to show God's love to anyone who was in need. A scruffy looking man came along asking for money for an operation for his sick elderly father. It seemed a genuine case, so I helped him out. A little while later he came asking for money to bury his father who had now, he told me, passed away. I was surprised to say the least when he turned up again to ask for money for medicine for his sick father. Needless to say that time he left empty handed. I began to realise that simply giving out money to everyone who asked was not necessarily the best use of limited resources. I needed to find a way of knowing which the genuine cases were.

As I looked around me at the overcrowded bamboo houses that seemed as though they were about to fall down any day, and saw the women washing clothes in the river, children with untreated skin infections and eleven year olds leaving school barely able to read, I longed to find ways to give some of them the hope of a better future.

I hoped the health promoters would help me find those I could best help. They knew the local people intimately, having lived with them all their lives. They knew who had resources, and who did not, who drank their money away and who worked hard to feed their family.

My first challenge was to convince these fine ladies, who were engrained with local myth and old wives tales that I knew what I was talking about, to gain their trust and confidence.

It was exciting when after a class where I taught them how to make re-hydration fluid for patients with diarrhoea, Hortencia came back recounting how she had taught her neighbours to make the drink and that their children who had had upset stomachs had got better.

It disappointed me when after teaching that injections were not necessary to get a common cold better; I heard that Nora had taken her husband for an antibiotic injection because he had a cold.

It astonished me how much faith they had in intravenous vitamin drips. It was common practice for people to ask for one to be applied whenever they felt unwell, weak or just tired. The local hospital put one up for every patient whether they had constipation or pneumonia. The ladies were incredulous that we did not do this in the UK. In their experience every doctor prescribed them; they were the panacea for those unexplainable symptoms, and the remedy for self-limiting maladies that would have improved with time alone.

The villagers thought the health promoters had gone loopy when they began to suggest eating a good vegetable soup instead of buying an expensive vitamin drip. When eventually the health promoters started to stick to this line, and refused to inject these costly, unnecessary drips I knew they were really starting to believe what I was teaching them. I felt exhilarated with the sense that I was achieving something. It made all the inconveniences of life sufferable.

## CHAPTER THREE

# Tree Climbing

My faithful companion in those early days was Ted Lancaster's book, "Setting Up Community Health Programmes." Following his advice I decided to carry out a health needs assessment of the families in the village to find out what their most pressing needs were. The health promoters and I set off from house to house with our questionnaires. It was a first class introduction to the people of the village and their way of life.

The village stretched five kilometres along a main road, and the houses were scattered into the countryside along small tracks. We set off visiting doused in insect repellent to ward off the mosquitoes, and with caps on our heads for protection from the sun.

The first hazard we encountered was the dogs. Every house had not just one, but several mutts that barked ferociously as we approached. This was not the place to be shy or intimidated. To be able to enter a house I had to yell at the top of my voice "Good morning neighbour" to get their attention so that they would call off the gnarling guard dogs. I also carried some stones secreted in my pockets ready to throw at any mutt that seemed too menacing.

As we reached the top of a hill seeking a far lying house, we had to climb a tree hastily to escape the jaws of a pack of dogs, and wildly wave and shout towards the house of the owners for a good ten minutes until someone noticed us and came to the rescue. Or maybe they just took their time as they were doubled up in stitches laughing at the comic spectacle of a white woman balanced precariously on the branch of their tree.

Once past the dogs the welcome was much warmer. The family invited us in and offered us a very sweet coffee. I just prayed the water had been boiled adequately and drank it down as best I could.

This family had eight children and they lived in a two roomed wooden house on stilts. I was amazed to see the children swung themselves down through the gaps in the floor boards instead of using the steps, laughing and playing. I was concerned about the state of overcrowding, and shocked to find such a large family had no toilet.

The next house we came to was made of split bamboo and plastic over a mud floor. In the damp climate such a house would not last more than a couple of rainy seasons before it collapsed. It saddened me greatly to see this elderly couple surviving under such an inadequate shelter, with no strength left to work to earn the money they needed to eat. These were the destitute. These were the neighbours God had brought me here to love. I wondered if I would be able to raise funds to build them a proper house, to let them live their final years in safety and dignity.

We met a fifty year old lady, Felicita, who had diabetes and was not on any treatment. She did not know what she should or should not be eating to help control her disease. She was self-medicating with a plant that they called "insulin", but she looked really unwell, and did not have the energy to care for her youngest son who was still at the village primary school. She herself was illiterate and she did not have the money to go and seek medical help. The family lived in a house loaned to them in return for looking after a small farm, and their only income was from the few chickens that they kept and a son who helped them as well as his own family.

I was stuck by her plight and determined to go back and find ways of helping her.

In the next house we found a forty year old man, Pablo, who had been left paralysed due to a polio infection he had contracted as a child. He was being looked after by his elderly father, as his mother had already died. He was lying in rags on a wooden board, painfully thin with a pressure sore over his sacrum, and his legs were contracted with smelly fungal infections in the skin creases. Wet rags were around his groin soaking up his urine, and flies bothered him constantly. I could not help but compare his tragic situation with the care he would have been receiving were he in the UK. I was shocked to see the state he was in. What I would have given to be able to simply 'phone a trusty district nurse to come and sort him out. As we left I chatted to Monserrat, feeling overwhelmed.

"Why does no one go and help them?" I asked.

"It is the family's responsibility." She responded. "Someone in the family should come and cook for them and bathe Pablo. If they had the money they could pay a nurse to come and care for him, but they are too poor for that."

"And could the neighbours not come and help?" I enquired.

"Neighbours will always help in a crisis," she agreed, "but he has been sick for years. It is too much of a burden for outsiders to keep helping for long periods of time. They have their own problems."

"What about the hospital? Would they help?" I wondered.

"They only help in emergencies. They would not receive someone in Pablo's condition. Only clinics, where you have to pay, would admit him."

We arrived at the next house where an elderly woman shared with us how her son had died recently from epilepsy.

"Juan started having fits when he was a boy. It was such a struggle for us. When we had money we bought his medicines, but there were many times we could not afford them. He had many fits. He was never able to work. Once he fell into the fire and was burnt. I could never leave him alone."

My mind was reeling as I took in the horror of a lifetime of suffering for the want of a few pills, when the lady started to cry. "Next door there is a young girl who has epilepsy. Sometimes I hear her thrashing about and it brings back memories of my son. I wish I had been able to look after him better. He was my company in the day. Now he is gone."

"Don't cry Señora," Monserrat admonished her gently; "You have to look to the future. Spend time with your grandchildren, help your daughter, and maybe we will be able to help the girl next door."

The old lady nodded gratefully, and we went on our way, hoping she would take our advice.

The girl next door was called Aida, and it was the same story, uncontrolled epilepsy and no money to buy the medicines. "I will come back and see how we can help you," I promised, deeply concerned for her plight. I could not just stand by and do nothing knowing that she was suffering for the simple lack of medicine.

The next family had six children crowded into a tiny house, and one of the boys had cerebral palsy. He was obviously intelligent, able to communicate with his family by sign language, and though he walked like a puppet on strings, he loved kicking a football around the yard. Monserrat confided that the family had been offered a place at a school for disabled children for the boy, but had declined as they preferred to take him in a wheelchair to beg on the streets of Santo Domingo.

He was a valuable source of income for them as he was. They saw no sense in educating him.

I had not imagined people might actually decline help they were offered, but seeing their desperate poverty could understand that they could think that it was more important to use the boy to put food on the table than to educate a child whom they probably thought would never be able to work.

In another rickety wooden house on stilts we found a ninety year old man with advanced Parkinson disease. He could no longer walk, so he sat on a contraption resembling a skateboard, almost on the floor, and whizzed around the house on these wheels. It was an ingenious, if interesting, alternative to a wheelchair.

We went past the witchdoctor's house, which had a queue of people waiting outside waiting to be seen. "Why do people go to see the witchdoctor?" I asked Monserrat.

"When people have broken bones or sprains they go for him to manipulate and set the bones, and give them herb compresses to use." She informed me. "They also use the witchdoctor for cleansings from bad spirits, or from curses, Mal Ojo, or Shock."

"What are they?" I asked puzzled by these maladies that I had never heard of before.

"Mal Ojo is when someone looks at you with evil intent. Shock is when a burst of bad air hits you and makes you ill." Monserrat explained.

"And how does the witchdoctor treat these conditions?" I enquired, intrigued.

"The witchdoctor passes an egg over you, and then opens the egg to diagnose such cases. If the egg is rotten you need cleansing. He then pours a mixture of alcohol made from sugar cane, and herbs over you and chants. He also uses cupping; making circular marks over your back with a cup. The witchdoctors in Santo Domingo are very famous. People come from all over the country to be treated by them." Monserrat informed me.

We took our leave, and I set off home. What we had witnessed was everyday life for Monserrat. For me it was wrong, unimaginable and heart breaking. It was a day that made me fall down on my knees and cry out to God for the suffering people I had met. It was a day that made me feel so ill-equipped and inadequate to meet the needs of all those I had encountered. It was a day that made me determined to reach out to these dear children of God.

As I returned to the spacious house I was renting, with its tiled floors and windows with glass in, I reflected on the conditions the people around me were living, the kaleidoscope of images I had witnessed dancing in my head. I tried to imagine having eight children and no washing machine. I wondered at the dangers of being exposed to mosquito bites night after night as the little blighters entered the houses at will. I shuddered at the parasites and bacteria having a field day in the children's stomachs as they had no adequate toilet and hand washing facilities. "I feel guilty that I have so much while those on my door step have so little." I agonised, "But I am hardly going to achieve anything by going to live in a shack. I'd probably just catch malaria and end up being airlifted home. I need to start to improve the living conditions of the people here. Maybe I cannot help everyone, but I can help some, one at a time. That is how to make a difference, while I still wait for my medical papers to come through. That is how I can be God's hands for these people."

# CHAPTER FOUR

# Mosquito Spraying

With the help of the health promoters I started with the mosquito problem.

We went to visit the local government's malaria department first, to request them to come and spray the houses in the village to kill the mosquitoes. This was an education for me in how one had to do such things in Ecuador. First we had to write a very flowery letter to the department with our petition.

Director
Malaria Department
Santo Domingo

Most honoured and respected Director, we do sincerely hope you are enjoying great success in life and good health. May you know every blessing in your work and in your family life.

We are writing to ask you most cordially and humbly if you would consider coming to our village, Nuevos Horizontes, to fumigate our houses against mosquitoes. We have suffered much illness as a result of mosquito bites and would be most grateful for your help.

Thanking you in anticipation of your positive response, we most gratefully leave this petition in your hands. May your daily endeavours bring you many rewards.

Yours faithfully

Village President, Village Secretary & Village Doctor.

The next job was to deliver the letter. This required a large group of people to go to present the letter in person to the Director of the malaria department so that he would be impressed that many people supported this request. I and the eight health promoters all climbed on the rickety ranchera to make the trip to town with the letter. On arrival at the malaria department we were ushered into the Director's office, which struck me as being just like a cartoon I had seen in a book about health care in developing countries. The Director lazed back in his chair with his feet on his desk, cigarette dangling from his mouth. He considered our letter as if he were about to do us the biggest favour in the world and then looked at the white woman through his slit-like eyes, calculating how much money he could get out of us. "Well," he considered out loud, "I have sufficient insecticide to use in your village, but I do not have any diesel to mix it with. So if you buy me twenty gallons of diesel, I will send my men to fumigate your village." The ladies with me whispered amongst themselves for a moment, then Nora negotiated with the Director that if they brought ten gallons he would do the job.

So the next task was to collect enough money to buy the requested diesel. We went back to the village and had to go around all the houses again to ask each family to contribute fifty cents towards the cost of the diesel. All those who contributed would have their house fumigated. I set off somewhat nervous as to what reception we would receive as we asked for the money.

"Doctorita it is great that you are organising this," the first father we came to exclaimed, "There are many mosquitoes at the moment, and my three daughters have all had dengue fever recently."

"I was in bed for a fortnight," his oldest daughter chipped in, "It was the most horrible feeling. I nearly died. I was all hot and cold and shivery and the pain! My head ached terribly and all my bones. I thought I was never going to get well again."

"I was most concerned about my youngest daughter," her father continued. "It was so scary to see her with fever day after day and night after night, and not to be able to do anything to lower it. I was beside myself. Thanks to God she eventually got better. We definitely need to get rid of these mosquitoes."

"I had malaria last month," his neighbour told us, "I was in bed for days shaking and unable to get warm. My head felt like it was going to burst. I could not work, and my wife had to go for medicines to the malaria department at the hospital. I thought I was going to die. I did not know how my wife was going to buy food while I was sick and unable to work. She had to go and find work washing clothes to survive. Here are my fifty cents, make sure you note me on the list."

"Oh yes we will definitely pay for that," said the administrator of the orphanage. "We are always so afraid the children will become sick from the mosquito bites. I had dengue fever once, and the pain and fever are indescribable. I cannot imagine little Victor going through that. I don't know that he would survive. Thank you for organising this spraying, it is really important."

Delighted at the positive response we were soon able to collect the money we needed and set off to a petrol station to buy the diesel. Then we headed back to the malaria department to deliver it. When we arrived the dollar signs in the Director's eyes got the better of him and he tried to insist we went and bought more diesel, but the ladies gave such a protest he realised he was not going to win that one, and backed down. I was glad I had the health promoters with me to handle these negotiations.

The order was given for the workers to come and fumigate our village the next day. The men who came were a great contrast to their boss. They laughed and joked and flirted all day long. "Doctorita, why are you still single at your age? Are the men in your country blind? I am single. Come out with me to a disco tonight. Do you like dancing?" "No, no, Doctorita, you don't want him, I am much more fun. Let me invite you to my birthday party on Saturday." "Have my phone number, call me any time." And so it went on the whole day long. I smiled and laughed with them politely, and inside was thinking, "Come on guys, give it a rest now, there is no way I am going to date an Ecuadorian, how can I change the subject?"

One of the villagers had loaned us his pickup for the day, so we raced around the houses with the workers looking like spacemen as they donned their masks and entered each house blasting the inside with their potion, then warning the dwellers not to go in again for a few hours. I shall never forget one house where there seemed to be a myriad of small children, and no adults around. The fumigator entered regardless and did his stuff, leaving a terrified huddle of youngsters on the doorstep too afraid to say anything. I wondered what account of their day they would give to their parents when they did return to the house. I think they thought aliens had visited them.

As the day drew a close, the men hopped sprightly on to the ranchera with their tanks to return home, and I went thankfully back to my house to put my feet up with a good cup of coffee (without sugar). I was pleasantly surprised to find that the insecticide had killed all not only the mosquitoes, but also the cockroaches in my house, so I was able to enjoy a few weeks without the repugnant black creatures crawling out of the kettle when I went to make a cuppa, or feeling one of them running over my chest after putting a T-shirt on. Bliss! It made the whole effort worth while.

It was an exhilarating feeling to have achieved so much, to know that the villagers were safe from the dangers of the mosquitoes for a good while. At last I was accomplishing something. But in the evenings, when I was alone in my house I could not help feeling lonely. Getting registered as a doctor was taking so much longer than I had expected. I felt dispirited. Everyone in the village married young and had their own families. There were no singles my age to hang out with in the evenings. I missed my good friends back home. I missed our chats and companionship. I missed their love and affection. People in the village were always astounded I was still single at my age, and constantly asking me why I did not marry. "How am I ever going to meet Prince Charming stuck out here in the back of beyond so far from civilization?" I asked myself. "I know anything is possible with God, but He is going to have a hard time arranging this one. Or maybe He is asking me to give up that dream. My head says He is sufficient, but my heart still feels the pain of separation and aloneness. I have to trust Him to give me the company I need."

A few days later, after our mosquito spraying success, it was a national bank holiday, Carnival. This took place the last two days before Lent. Everyone had these days off work, and went on mass to the beaches, swimming pools and rivers - anywhere there was water. In the streets families set up paddling pools for their children to play in and threw buckets of water over passers-by. Selling water pistols was big business. As I looked on the whole city went crazy.

It was impossible to go out of the orphanage gate without getting wet, and impossible to get into town against the flow of the traffic. The city emptied and everyone went in search of a river or swimming pool. One either had to join in, or stay indoors. In the heat no one minded being wet all day, and everyone threw themselves into enjoying the fun as much as possible. It was a mad few days of water fights and barbeques. I decided it was time to have some fun and turned the hose on the orphans. They ran in all directions, squealing with delight and giving as good as they got.

At lunchtime we had a barbequed chicken pieces and pork ribs, accompanied by rice and grilled bananas. We all sat around, soaking wet, the fat dripping down our chins, licking our fingers. Janet fed Victor his soup with great patience, skilfully getting it into him despite his tense jaw muscles. "Let's go out and buy some barbequed cows guts this afternoon," the orphans clamoured, "They are cooking some just down the road. Please, please," they cried.

"Have you ever tried them?" they asked me.

"No, I have to confess I have not," I replied with a shudder.

"Come and try some," they clamoured, so, reluctantly, I obliged, and despite feeling my face must be turning green I gamely chewed on the offering, as cars drove past us chucking water in our direction. I could not say in all honesty it was a snack I would be rushing to eat again soon. It was decidedly chewy. But at least it took me out of myself and I gladly embraced the fun and company.

That evening I escaped to visit Mary for some British pancakes. It was Shrove Tuesday after all. I savoured them with the fresh taste of lemon plucked from a tree in the garden. "It is so nice to eat something vaguely normal," I commented to Mary.

"You must come any time you wish," she assured me kindly, "there is usually something on the go here."

Ash Wednesday saw many people attending Catholic mass, and walking around with ash on their foreheads. Everyone went back to work, and it was possible to get about without fear of a bucket of water being thrown in your direction.

Shaking my head at the inexplicable craziness of the previous few days, I too went back to work.

Needing to keep occupied and spurred on by the success of our mosquito-killing efforts, the health promoters and I turned our attention to the lack of toilets in the village. We went to the government department for water and sewage, MIDUVI, with a suitably flowery letter requesting help. This was to prove a tougher nut to crack. They received the letter in the MIDUVI office, however then we had to go back again and ask if there was any response to our request at least ten times. Eventually we were told our request would be put forward for the following year's budget. It was becoming clear our toilet project was not going to receive funding from this source.

So I turned my attention to helping some of the individuals whom we had discovered in the census with chronic illnesses who were not receiving medical care. Monserrat and I went to visit Aida who was living with epilepsy. In her twenties, she suffered frequent fits. She had had epilepsy since birth, after she was deprived of oxygen during a difficult delivery in the jungle. She had learning difficulties, which were worsening with the ongoing seizures. She bore the scars of accidents her fits had caused her to have. Once she had fallen into a fire. Her family could never leave her by herself.

She was seated on a fallen log with her five girl cousins and her Aunt. They were making some pretty purses, hand embroidered with beautiful tones and colours.

"When was the last time you had a check-up?" I asked Aida.

"Oh she has not seen a doctor for many years," her Aunt reported. "We just buy her medicines when we can. Here is what she is taking."

"This is too small a dose for her now," I explained. "The dose should be increased as she grows."

"But we cannot always find the money for the tablets anyway," Aida's aunt said sadly.

Her cousin chimed in, "You see Doctorita we are five sisters, all going to school, and our father left us two years ago. If we go and seek him out he sometimes gives us something, but he does not give our Mum any regular help towards our food, clothes and education. Our Mum slaves all day every day. She cuts the bananas that grow on our small piece of land to sell them, she goes and washes clothes for the neighbours, she tries to sell clothes from catalogues in the community, but we just manage to scrape by. We all try to help as well, but we are studying, and we so want to be able to finish our education, to be able to make something of ourselves. We take care of our cousin Aida, but there just is not the money to buy her medicines, however hard we try."

"How often does she have seizures?" I asked sobered by this sad reality.

"She has them almost every day, to tell the truth. To be honest she is hardly ever taking medicine."

"And can you not do something to make your father help you out more?" I asked, concerned for them all.

"We are afraid of him. He is a violent man. We are glad he does not live here anymore because he maltreated our mother. If he sees her in town he stalks her and threatens her. We only go and find him when we are really desperate, and even then he makes us feel like dirt before he gives us anything."

I sadly wondered how to help them. I could recommend the correct dosages of the medicine she should be taking, but what could I do about the real problem: the cost of affording the pills for the months and years to come.

I could help them by buying the medicines this month, but this was not a sustainable answer to the problem either. Funds were limited and there must be many people needing the same help. Also I did not want to make them dependent on outsiders.

"I want to help you Aida," I told her, "but I am going to have to think about how we can manage to raise the money you need to buy your medicines. There must be some way of doing it. I will come and visit you again soon." I promised as I left, perplexed as to the best way forward, but determined to help this damaged girl who was so precious to Jesus.

I could see that chronic illness was a big problem for the patient and their whole family. It caused a tremendous economic burden for the family. Not only could the sick person often not contribute financially to the income of the family, they also cost so much in the medicines they needed.

Next Monserrat and I went to visit Felicita, the lady we had met with diabetes. We chatted to her about diabetes, the risks to her health and her need to take care of herself. Her husband was concerned for her, and wanted to know what he could do to help her.

"She needs to be very careful about what she eats," I explained, "She cannot eat any sugar, no fizzy drinks, and no sugar in her coffee. She needs to eat plenty of vegetables and not too much rice, manioc and bananas – just small portions."

"I can have brown sugar though can't I? That does no harm," queried Felicita.

"No, no, not even brown sugar." I remonstrated, "That is just as bad in diabetes. You need to take medicines as well to lower the sugar in your blood."

"But Doctorita, my wife is taking the insulin plant," countered her husband. "She does not need to take any chemical medicines."

As we chatted to them in their plain board house on stilts, with windows open to the elements, they agreed to us checking her blood sugar. It was very high. She was adamant she did not want medicines, so we agreed to come back and visit again another day to see if her blood sugar came down with the insulin plant.

When I returned to the orphanage, Janet was waiting for me with little Victor. He had caught a cold and was very wheezy. "Doctorita please help Victor," cried Janet. "I am so afraid he will not be able to breathe."

Little Victor tried valiantly to give his winning smile, despite feeling so unwell, as I found the nebuliser and began to treat him. He relaxed as the medicine took effect and soon fell asleep exhausted. Another of the orphans, Lucia approached, caressed his forehead gently, and began to sing to him. I knew Lucia had been kept chained in a box prior to her rescue, victim of abuse and violence. Since her rescue she had undergone several operations for cleft palate and was partially deaf. It brought a lump to my throat to see these two children comforting each other with such affection. They were trophies of God's grace.

As I observed this example of the lives of children with chronic illness being transformed I wanted to find ways of extending this help to those living in the community, to epileptics like Aida and diabetics like Felicita. They were important to God as well.

It was time to pay another visit to Felicita. She looked tired and lacked the energy to do much. She sat on the porch and watched the chickens running around her rather listlessly as Monserrat and I approached. When we checked her blood sugar it was just as high as before. To my delight she and her husband agreed to try using the medicines they were so wary of. This time I gave them to her for free, and explained carefully how she should take them. Neither she nor her husband could read the instructions. I hoped with all my heart that the next time we went she would be feeling better, that she would allow me to help her.

When I went back to visit Felicita I was delighted to indeed find her feeling so much better. Monserrat checked her blood sugar and it had come down nicely. "Come and visit me once a month," I instructed Felicita, "and I will give you more medicine each time."

"Yes, yes Doctorita", promised Felicita. "I will come without fail and thank you so much.

"Excellent", I thought to myself as I walked home. "At last we are winning the battle."

I felt so frustrated that I could not yet start attending patients as a registered doctor. I decided it was time for a trip to Quito to the University to ask about the papers again in person. I was determined not to be put off again this time.

"Señora Margarita, good day," I began politely, "What news do you have for me?" I asked.

"Doctorita, what a pleasure to see you," Margarita replied, equally politely. "I am afraid there is still no news. Come again next week and ask."

"I think it is time I spoke to the Rector to find out what the delay is." I stated firmly. "It is almost a year since I gave you my documents and there appears to be no progress at all. Please ask the Rector if I can speak to him."

Margarita went off, and came back claiming the Rector was occupied at present. "Then I shall wait until he has a few minutes free to speak to me." I claimed, taking a seat. "I am not going back to Santo Domingo until he gives me the honour of an audience with him."

Half an hour later I was ushered in to the great man's office.

"There seems to be a problem with the revalidation of my medical degree," I observed, going straight to the point, "So I would like you to explain to me what the problem is."

"Well, Doctora, your medical certificate says you are Bachelor in medicine, and that is the title we use for high school graduates, not university graduates."

At last I had found the reason for the delay. "But that is the title we use in Britain when graduating from University." A bright idea struck me. "Doctor, your university revalidated the degree of a British colleague of mine two years ago. Would it be possible to find her papers? There you will see the same title, Bachelor."

A short while later we were looking at the papers of my colleague and the Rector had to agree I was right. "OK," he assured me, "We will now provide your revalidation papers. Come again in a fortnight and they will be ready."

Hardly daring to believe it might actually be true, I returned to Santo Domingo hope revived. "Thank you, thank you, thank you," I breathed, "At last I can start the work I have felt called to for so long. Oh please may it be true this time!"

Felicita stopped coming to see me. Disappointed and concerned, I decided to go and visit her again to find out what had happened. "Good day Doctorita," she greeted me unblushingly. "Good day Señora Felicita," I replied. "Are you well? You have stopped coming for your medicines."

"My mother is now taking these natural remedies," her daughter explained. "The man who came and sold them to us said they would cure her. Your medicines can only control the disease, not cure it."

My heart sank as I realised they had been taken in by this charlatan. "How are you feeling?" I enquired. "Do you feel any better?"

"Well, I do feel somewhat thirsty and tried," Felicita admitted grudgingly, "but the man promised me these would cure me."

I suggested we check her blood sugar, and it was sky high again. The family sat together soberly, taking in the death of their dream of a cure. Felicita started coming for medicines again. A church in the UK started covering the cost of her medicines each month. I hoped she understood that diabetes was a long term condition that was not going to simply disappear. I hoped this time she would keep coming.

Aida came to see me with her five cousins. "Doctorita, good day" they greeted me. "How are you all?" I asked them, pleased to see them, welcoming them into my house. I was still puzzling over how to help Aida long term in her predicament of needing epilepsy medications.

"We have come to show you these purses we have made." They told me holding out a handful of exquisitely embroidered offerings. "We make them together, and were wondering if there would be any way of selling them to help pay for Aida's medicine."

"What I good idea," I responded enthusiastically, "I am sure there are people in my country who would love to buy a purse like this. We should definitely be able to sell some."

I paid them up front for the purses, and sent them to my Mum to sell for us in Scotland. I sent the girls home to make some more, and Aida started taking her medicine consistently. It was wonderful to see how proud they were to be able to earn the money themselves for the medicine, instead of receiving a hand out. It was a real boost to their self-confidence and self-worth. "I think this could be the start of something," I meditated happily, delighted at this solution to the problem. "This idea has great potential."

## CHAPTER FIVE

# Queen Elizabeth

"Will the papers finally be ready?" I asked myself constantly as I rode the bus to Quito on tenterhooks. At last, the answer was "Yes." I held my revalidated medical degree in my hands with a great sense of relief. Finally I could start work as a doctor. Finally I could put to use all my training and preparation. Finally I could seek to alleviate suffering and cure the sick. My dream was at last coming true.

Ecuadorean law required I first complete an obligatory year in a government health centre before I could practice independently.

After a few weeks and several more trips to Quito I was allocated to the main health centre in Santo Domingo. The director there was a friendly chap, Dr. Jaramillo. "Good day Doctora," he greeted me. "Where are you from?"

"I am from England," I replied, wondering if he knew where that was.

"Sent by Queen Elizabeth!" He exclaimed jokingly. "I am very pleased to see you. I need a doctor in the paediatric outpatients department. What brings you to Ecuador? Are you married?"

"I have come to work for a charity," I explained, "and I am single."

"But how can that be? A beautiful woman like you? The men in your country must be blind! Are you interested in dating an Ecuadorean man? We are very good looking you know."

I was starting to feel annoyed at the direction this conversation was going. "No I don't want to go out with you smarmy Ecuadoreans," I felt like shouting to the rooftops. "Why can't you just stick to the subject in hand?" Instead I plastered a polite smile on my face and "When do I start work?" I asked, changing the subject decidedly.

"I need you straight away, my Queen Elizabeth." He told me with alacrity. "Come at eight o'clock on Monday."

"Crumbs," I thought to myself, "I never wanted to be Queen; Doctor was all I was trying to get recognised as!" But seeing as he seemed to be in a good mood, I took a deep breath and decided to take the plunge. "Dr Jaramillo," I began respectfully, "I have been here for a year already and have trained some health promoters in the village of New Horizons, where there is no government health centre. Would it be possible for me to attend patients there as well?"

I held my breath as I waited for his response. I had waited so long already to be able to help these villagers, was there any chance he would let me start in earnest now? Or was I going to have to wait for another year?

"Hmm Queen Elizabeth, let me think. You do have a case as it is true we have no health centre out that way. There are many villages that direction and it is hard for them to make the journey into town to find a doctor when they are ill. I should also take into account you are offering your services to us for free. How about this? You work here in paediatrics Monday to Wednesday and out in the village Thursday and Friday."

"That would be wonderful, thank you," I replied a huge grin on my face. "It will be great to be able to continue working with the villagers as well. You are most kind."

"Not at all, now make sure you are not late on Monday. You have to clock in and out to fulfil the requirements of the government service year."

"Wow," I thought as I made my way home, "I never imagined he would let me keep working in the village as well. This is much better than I had dared hoped for. Excellent! Excellent!" Monday, my official start as a doctor in Ecuador could not come soon enough.

Work in the Health Centre in town was very different to anything I had experienced before and very different to what I was expecting. I had thought I would just turn up and be able to help each needy person that came to see me, when in reality there were many obstacles and hurdles to be tackled. It was to be a hard year.

Patients came from the poorest parts of town, queuing up at day break to be first in line and obtain an appointment, needing the free medicines supposed to be on offer. Patients were attended in the order they had arrived. I was allocated a room and left to get on with it. There was no scope for influencing the system. No one was interested in doing a better job. I was surprised at how few appointments they gave out each day. I had to clock in and out for my obligatory eight hours a day, but was only expected to attend twenty five patients in that time, and only these official patients could receive the free medicines.

Each morning I settled down expectantly for the stream of small patients waiting to see me. I tried to help each of them the best I could in the circumstances; these tiny people who reminded me of the little ones who had stolen my heart that summer long before.

Little Juan's mother brought me the worms he had passed in a jar to show me. Having successfully despatched him with worm medicine I vowed to take it myself on a regular basis just in case, as I never wanted to see one of those slimy, wriggly creatures coming out of one of my bodily orifices.

Yanela's mother brought in her nappy with disgustingly smelly diarrhoea inside, in the hopes that this offering would enlighten me as to the cause of her problem. I gagged as I disposed of it in the bin and hurriedly prescribed her rehydration fluids which, I assured her, would cure her in no time.

Many babies sported a red bead bracelet to ward off evil spirits and illnesses. Sometimes they allowed me to pray for them instead, asking God for protection for their little one.

All the mothers wanted me to give their child vitamin drops, even when the free hospital supply ran out and it would cost them considerable sums of money to buy them. They believed this would make their child abound with appetite and grow delightfully chubby. I urged them to feed their child plenty of fruit and vegetables, but the sad reality was they did not have the money to buy them.

Lesli was brought in with a runny nose, red pus filled eyes and a hacking cough. She had a cloth nappy tied on with a plastic bag covering it. Her skin had been invaded by impetigo. It was frustrating not to be able to do anything about the real cause of her problems; the inadequate housing and water supply, the overcrowding and lack of sewage facilities, the poverty and lack of a balanced diet.

"Aren't you Andrea?" Her mother asked me. I looked at her more closely, recognising her as one of the children who had played with us in the slum ten years previously. She had cut her arm and I had bandaged it one afternoon as we sat in the dirty street. She remembered my name. After all that time she remembered my name. My heart missed a beat. Carmen, her name came back to me as well. Her mother had been a prostitute I remembered. Carmen was now a mother herself, but was still living in the same poverty and ignorance as her parents. How my heart grieved for her, and longed to be able to change things for her daughter's generation. This spiral of unnecessary suffering had to stop. I impulsively got up from my chair and gave Carmen a heartfelt hug, and a kiss to little Lesli; blessings from their Heavenly Father who longed to see them well and whole. Then we turned to the matter in hand.

"Have you been bathing your baby?" I asked Carmen.

"No Andrea," she responded emphatically, "I do not want her to catch cold and pneumonia."

"But she is dirty and that is making her sicker Carmencita," I remonstrated, frustrated at this common belief that you should not bath a child who had a cold. "Heat up some water and bath her inside your house with plenty of soap," I instructed. "That will stop Lesli developing pneumonia and help heal up her sores."

"But you are going to give me some vitamins aren't you Andrea?" She replied, not seeming to take on board my advice at all.

"Yes I will give you some, but you must bath little Lesli as well."

I gave her an antibiotic and some eye ointment, and showed her how to put it in Lesli's eyes. I also gave her some soap to bath her with, and the vitamins she wanted. She left giving me another long hug in memory of that summer so long before and promised she would bring Lesli back again soon for a check-up. As I watched her go I was glad I had kept my promise and returned to

Ecuador. I whispered a silent prayer for protection for that little family, and hoped with all my heart I could make a difference to these young families, despite the overwhelming magnitude of their problems.

Next in was Jorge. I was puzzled when his mother sat down and pronounced, "He needs help Doctorita, because he has "Pujos" (pushing)."

"Forgive me Mother," I exclaimed, "But I have not heard of this illness before. What is it?"

"Well Jorge has started straining his tummy because he saw a woman pregnant with a female baby." She explained, obviously astonished that I did not know about this problem. "I have jumped over him three times, and taken him to the witchdoctor for cleansing, but he is no better, so I have brought him to you." She paused expectantly as I searched my imagination for some wise remedy to this problem. "Perhaps she is expecting me to wave a magic wand or recommend a magic potion," I joked to myself.

I resorted to checking Jorge was not actually constipated then gave some general feeding advice, as I figured whatever the problem really was it was probably self-resolving, or just a little wind. I do not think Jorge's Mum left impressed with the white doctor.

The next patient was a new born baby. I noticed he had a strip of cloth wrapped firmly round his middle to make his umbilicus form nicely. Ecuadoreans had a real fear of their child ending up with a sticking out tummy button, as it was considered very ugly. For this reason they filled the umbilicus with cotton wool balls, and bound their tummies for the first month or more, to make sure the tummy button formed prettily. This baby had a fungal infection in his umbilicus due to the humidity, but his indignant mother did not take kindly to my advice that she should leave his tummy button uncovered.

The pharmacy assistant popped in to see me. "Cross fungal cream and vitamins off your list, Doctora, they have now run out." She informed me, very matter of fact.

"But what can I give the patients now?" I asked her concerned I now had no remedies to offer the patients.

"You just have to give them the prescription to go and buy in a pharmacy. We will not get more supplies for at least another three months."

It seemed so brusque and callous, but it was just the way it was, and there was nothing I could do to magic up more medicines either. Tearful and frustrated, I called in the final patient of the day.

The two month old girl had the appearance of Turner's syndrome. To receive attention from specialists I had to tell her sixteen year old mother to go to Quito to the children's hospital there. This involved paying for the bus journey, finding somewhere to stay, and going early in the morning to get an appointment to be seen later in the day. I do not know if that young girl ever made the trip to get an accurate diagnosis for her baby. If she did not have family support behind her it would have been almost impossible for her.

As I was leaving I bumped into my boss. "So how are you finding the paediatric department Queen Elizabeth?" He asked me. "They tell me you are despatching the patients in record time."

"Well, they mostly all have the same common problems," I commented, hoping he did not think I was doing a bad job.

"Tomorrow you will be in the village won't you? Make sure you bring a list of all the patients you attend back with you on Monday."

"Yes boss," I smiled, "See you later."

I felt very ineffective in my work in the health centre. The realities of poverty, ignorance and lack of resources were bigger beasts than I had thought to reckon with. Despite now having my medical papers I was still not free to help people as I wanted. Feeling despondent I went to have a chat with Mary. "Mary it is so frustrating, I don't feel like I am helping anyone," I complained. "Most of the children have common illnesses like worms, coughs and diarrhoea, but the medicines for these have now run out, and anyway the real problem is their poor living conditions. Added to this all I can do for those that have a more serious problem is recommend they go to Quito. But how can they go when they have no money to pay for the bus fare or to pay for a hostel to stay in?"

"You can only do what is within the realms of possibility," Mary consoled me. "You can't expect to be able to help everybody. It is just not realistic. The whole system needs to change. You have to look for those opportunities where you can make a difference to someone: even save a life."

"The people in the town are different from those here in the village," I reflected, "They arrive frustrated, tired and demanding. Today I got annoyed with a mother who found her way to my window while I was attending a patient in my room, and was insisting I attend to her baby through the window as she had not managed to get a slot that day. It seemed such a rude interruption to me. She had no regard for the privacy of the patient I was already attending nor was she willing to wait her turn. But then she had probably been up since four in the morning, was desperate for someone to help her with her sick baby and was just trying to get some attention. I should not have got cross with her."

"You will get used to it, you are just beginning. A lot of what you are feeling is still due to you being out of your culture and getting used to a new one. You will find ways of helping people like that mother today. It is normal to react badly sometimes. It is all so different from the organised appointment systems in England. Interruptions are a way of life here and people don't worry about privacy so much. You are still adapting to the culture here," Mary pointed out. "You just have to stick at it."

Digging deep, and determined not to be beaten by these frustrations, I went home to draw some leaflets to educate the mothers I was seeing daily on how to care for their sick children. I scraped together all the medicines I could get my hands on so that I would not have to send the children away empty handed. Maybe it was not much in the scheme of things, but I could not just sit back and do nothing.

Just then Monserrat arrived at the door looking for me to ask me to come and speak to some cousins of hers who had a sick baby. We went to the house, and I discovered they had a little baby boy, just a few days old, who had a heart defect which was making him blue through lack of oxygen. In the hospital in Santo Domingo they had had him on oxygen in an incubator, but they had told the parents they would have to take him to Quito for a heart operation. The parents had decided to take their baby home to be baptised and then to let him die as the prospect of trying to pay for such treatment seemed to them an insurmountable obstacle.

However, when after a few hours of being home their baby had not yet died they were having second thoughts and wondering if they should try and seek further help. I took the tiny baby in my arms and silently prayed for the words to convince his parents to at least give him the chance of life. I explained as best I could the possibility that surgery could save this precious child's life. The parents listened intently, hope regenerating in their hearts. With the support of Monserrat and others in their extended family, they finally agreed it was worth making the trip to at least find out more in the specialist hospital in Quito. We took the little baby back to the incubator and oxygen in the local hospital. Everyone chipped in to pay for the ambulance, and the next morning the baby and his parents set off for Quito. In the end we heard that after going to four different hospitals in search of someone who could do the required operation, that baby's life was saved. The parents returned home very happy to have their tiny son alive, despite the debts they had yet to pay off for his life saving surgery.

"This is what I came to do," I exclaimed, "Save lives and help people. This is the kind of medicine I love." This was what made being in Ecuador worthwhile. Being in the right place at the right time, available to intervene and lend a helping hand. I hoped working in the village would allow me to really get to know my patients and their circumstances, to help them tackle some of the root causes of their problems. I hoped I would be accepted and listened to. I hoped the villagers would see the love of God through my life and work.

## CHAPTER SIX

# Seeds of Hope

Back in the village we had formally finished the course for the health promoters, and were ready to start work. We had the use of a room lent to us by the orphanage, beside a dentist who already offered her services there to the community. It was time to celebrate the year of learning together and to demonstrate to the villagers that the ladies had studied. We organised a presentation of certificates to the health promoters during a community meeting. I was excited at this momentous occasion; this beginning of what I hoped would be the transforming of people's lives.

We began by explaining some posters we had made about the importance of healthy eating and exercise, and the dangers of smoking and alcohol. Next, with great pride, I presented each health promoter with her certificate, amidst much applause and appreciation from the villagers. We took lots of photos of the health promoters with their families, as they posed in their newly made white coats full of anticipation at their new role. I was so happy to see them proud of all they had learnt and full of confidence.

I took the chance to explain that we would be starting to attend patients each Thursday and Friday in the village, inviting people to come along and spread the word amongst their neighbours, as I needed enough people to come along to justify my days there to the great Dr Jaramillo.

The villagers wanted to build a health centre for us to work in, so after the meeting Mary sold some homemade cakes to raise money for the building fund. I was helping to serve the tempting slices of chocolate and vanilla cake, when a rather eye-catching young man called Vladimir approached and jokingly asked, "Is the Doctorita for sale?" flashing me a wide grin. I just gave a small smile and sighing dismissed the comment as another of those rather ridiculous flirtations that I never took seriously. I turned to the next cake client and promptly forgot about the incident. Vladimir wandered off with his slice of cake, plotting ways to get to know me better.

I was filled with anticipation at being able to officially start work in the village. Here, surely, I would be able to make a real difference to people; to cure the children and alleviate the suffering of the elderly. I wanted to show the love and compassion of Jesus, to point my new neighbours to Him.

Working in the village was certainly a breath of fresh air in comparison to the long days in town. I was free to organise things as I wished, and we were relaxed and informal. At first there were not many patients as people were still wary of the new doctor, wondering if I knew what I was talking about and how much medicines would cost them. I knew I would have to be patient and that it would take time to gain people's confidence. I noted down everyone I could conceivably count as a patient on the list I had to present to my boss, not wanting him to turn round and say I could no longer spend time there.

When there were no patients to attend I chatted to the health promoters working with me, and we drank plenty of cups of herbal tea to pass the time. We talked about their families and their hopes for their children.

"Do all your family live here?" I asked them.

"Most of them," Monserrat replied, "Our parents and children and many aunts and uncles do. I have a niece in Spain though, and Hortencia has family in Colombia still."

"Do you not miss your family back home?" They asked me. "How long do you think you will stay in Ecuador for? I should think your parents want you to go back soon."

"Yes I miss them," I answered, "But I am enjoying my time here too. I am only just beginning. You won't get rid of me yet. I haven't lived with my parents since I went to University."

"Our children only leave home once they marry, and even then sometimes they still live with us at first, or just build a little house next door. It must be very lonely to come so far from home. Do you not mind living alone? Why don't you get married? We would be too afraid to live all by ourselves."

"Well, I guess I am used to it, I have lived alone for several years now. I will only marry if I find a good man." I asserted.

"We have some good sons," they assured me enthusiastically, "We must introduce you."

I just laughed pleasantly. Much as I desired the companionship and love of a husband, I was looking for a well-educated, like-minded man, who could make interesting conversation; someone who would cherish and protect me, someone who would make me feel special and beautiful, someone who had a heart to serve God and his neighbour. I doubted there was someone like that in the village.

Vladimir, came into the health centre bringing an elderly lady to see me. "Good day Doctora," he greeted me with his wide grin and a carefully placed kiss on the cheek. "My neighbour is unwell, so I have brought her to see you as I am sure you will be able to help her."

I knew I had seen him before somewhere, but it was a few moments before I remembered, "Of course, this is the guy who wanted to buy me at the cake sale. Well, it is nice of him to bring his neighbour along for help."

"Bring her straight in," I responded and set about finding out what ailed her. Vladimir waited outside, determined to also make the most of kissing me good bye, and plotting how else he could gain my attention.

"Who is that young man?" I asked Monserrat casually once they had gone.

"Oh he is Vladimir, the oldest son of a good friend of mine. They are a lovely family, always helping other people, and Vladimir has even managed to study at University. I believe he is working as an Engineer now," she commented as I filed away the information for future reference, somewhat impressed despite myself.

The health promoters did a great job helping me look after the patients who came along, advertising our services amongst the villagers, and looking out for those who needed help. One of the greatest privileges was being able to go and visit patients in their own homes. It enabled me to see what they really needed and to meet the whole family. Such visits were the start of friendships that were to last for years. They were times when heaven opened and touched earth. They were times when I glimpsed eternity.

One day Monserrat asked if we could go and visit a young man who had suffered an accident a couple of years previously, and was now paralysed. He lived in a village thirty minutes' drive into the countryside on an unmade road. We set off one afternoon to visit him. Jeovhanny was married with two beautiful daughters, aged eleven and thirteen, who had long tight curls framing their sculptured faces. They lived in a wooden house on stilts and owned a little land, two milking cows and some chickens. He was quadriplegic, unable to move his arms or legs, confined to a bed and dependent on his wife and daughters to attend to his every need. He even had a tracheotomy through which they administered suction and oxygen when chest secretions built up making it difficult for him to breathe or to eat. They could never leave him alone in the house.

"Wow this woman does an amazing job of caring for her husband," I thought to myself as I looked at his spotlessly clean skin and the fresh bed with no evidence of the incontinence he suffered. Alicia attended him day and night, as well as trying to make enough money from milking the cows and selling eggs to feed the family. Since leaving the hospital two years previously they had had no visit or help from a health professional. She did a truly remarkable job of caring for him.

Alicia told us, "Jeovhanny was in hospital for a year in Quito after his accident. I had to sell our truck to pay for his treatment, so we were left without a livelihood. Our daughters could not go to school during that year. I always need one of them to be here with me as I cannot leave Jeovhanny alone."

"You do an amazing job of looking after him." I commented.

"I was with him the whole year in the hospital. I learnt how to look after him from the nurses there." She replied, justifiable pride in her voice.

As we sat there on the hard board bed, with its thin mattress, and sacks filled with clothing for pillows, I thought about how I could help this man and his family. I wondered what made Alicia sacrifice so much, day in and day out, to serve her husband. I could hear God's whisper to help this family whom He always had in His sight, and to do so was a joy.

First I started with Jeovhanny, who spent all his time lying down in bed. I encouraged him to try sitting up supported on soft pillows little by little so he became accustomed to being upright again. At first he felt dizzy when he tried it, but as time went by when I went to visit him he would be sitting up in bed, looking much brighter. "Hi Jeovhanny, today I have something new for you to try," I greeted him. "This is going to be a great workout for your arms to build up their strength. You should be able to do lots more if you can move them more." I told him enthusiastically. I rigged up a pulley with stones in socks hung off one end so he could do some exercises with his arms.

"This is a great idea," he exclaimed, "I am going to try and lift heavier and bigger stones."

"Exactly," I encouraged him. "With practice I think you should be able to learn to feed yourself."

I could not imagine what it must be like for a once active and hardworking man to now be confined to bed, unable to do even the simplest tasks for himself. Bored and helpless, his world had become so small. I loved visiting the family. They were so isolated and abandoned. They welcomed the company, the medical help and the practical suggestions. They became friends and made the most of all the help they received.

Don Sofonias's case was so different. He was a frail, very thin man of about seventy years. He had worked in the orphanage in the gardens as they had helped him by giving him a job. He had worked well past retirement age, as was the custom for older folk in the village. He had no pension and needed the income. He lived with his two single sons, who drank all their money. Perhaps as there was no woman to help them, Don Sofonias wandered around in dirty clothes and appeared to survive on biscuits and coca cola. Despite both he and his sons having had regular income for years their house was tumbling down. He often came along asking us to give him remedies for minor complaints until one day we received the news he had suffered a stroke.

I went to visit him with some of the health promoters. He was lying in a urine soaked bed, with paralysis down one side of his body. The cane house he lived in was built on stilts, with the sloping wooden floor at the point of giving way completely. Mary and the health promoters did a wonderful job in the days that followed helping to clean him and his bed, taking him meals, and trying to ensure he took the medications I prescribed him. It was wonderful to watch the team responding to his need in such a dedicated fashion. They truly showed him the love and compassion of Jesus as they cleaned up his incontinence and fed him soup with infinite patience. But we were never going to be able to effect real change in his situation.

Don Sofonias' daughters appeared from time to time to load him up into a neighbour's lorry and take him off to healers whom they believed would be able to work a miracle cure. However his recovery was gradual. Eventually he got back on his feet and started walking up and down the road through the village again. The sight of him slowly limping along with a long stick he had fashioned from a handy tree became a familiar one.

He limped down to the local school at break time so that they would give him some breakfast and then on to his daughter's for lunch. Despite our best efforts we never managed to get him to take his medicines regularly. Those he did not feel any immediate benefit from he did not believe were helping him, so they were left discarded around the house. Similarly he never managed to do sufficient exercises with his weak arm, resisting our attempts to help him, and gradually it became more and more fixed in a bent position.

I was called out of the health centre to attend him as he had just fallen suffering a brief seizure. "Monserrat, help me lift him, that's it, let's get him inside."

"Doctor why don't you give him a vitamin drip to increase his strength so he does not keep having seizures?" His daughter asked me as her father recovered.

"I'm sorry but a vitamin drip would not do any good." I replied patiently. "He needs to take his medicines. I gave him some last week to control the seizures, and when Monserrat went to visit him she found them all by his bed - he hadn't taken any of them."

"Doctor I know you are doing your best but I think he needs injections not tablets. Off we go Dad, you look like you are able to make it home again now."

"Oh dear Monserrat, what are we going to do?" I asked her. "He needs to be nursed, to do his arm exercises and to have three square meals a day, not vitamin injections."

"It is the family's responsibility though Doctorita." Monserrat reminded me. "You cannot take over or force things upon them."

He always seemed such a neglected old man, predeceased by his wife, and living in such squalor and filth. But I struggled to know how much to help. The health promoters were happy to help in a crisis, and did so at personal sacrifice, but warned against making him dependent on outsiders, when in their view the responsibility to look after him lay with his family. It certainly was difficult to help him when he did nothing to help himself, and when his view of what he needed was so different to mine. But I felt guilty and frustrated when I saw this man whom Jesus died for so unkempt and uncared for.

In contrast there seemed so many ways to be able to help Jeovhanny. They used all they were given and made such an effort to help themselves. I asked a local carpenter to make a table for Jeovhanny to go on his bed over his legs, with a hole in it for his bowl to go in. With the help of splints attaching a spoon to his arm he started to practice feeding himself. "You should watch this film," I told him as I gave him a copy of the Joni film to inspire him. "It is the true story of a woman left quadriplegic by a diving accident, and shows her recovery, rehabilitation, fortitude and faith."

"Thank you for the film," he grinned the next time I visited. "We borrowed the DVD player from the neighbours and all watched it together. What happened to Joni is just like what has happened to me. She has her spinal fracture a little higher than mine, but she can do so much after her rehabilitation. I must keep practising."

I came away from visiting Jeovhanny thinking, "This is what my work here is all about. It is such fun to be able to think of creative ways to help the family. I have such admiration for the great job they are doing in such terrible circumstances. It is a pleasure to be able to help them."

I made Jeovhanny's needs known in the UK, and was delighted to receive a donation for them. I bought them some pink anthurium plants. Their tropical blooms were sought after by florists. Alicia planted them in their garden. Looking after the plants was easy work for her and the girls. They picked the flowers produced by the plants each week and sold them to florists, giving them a little more regular income.

"Now this is what I call being a holistic doctor," I smiled to myself, very pleased at how it was possible to give a boost to this hard working family. "I really feel like I am making a difference to this family. It gives me such joy."

My only concern was that the girls did not appear to be attending school. Something to tackle on the next visit, I made a mental note.

Not so good was the next visit from Don Sofonias' daughter. Don Sofonias admittedly was improving, nature was taking its course and each day he was able to walk a little further and gained a little strength. "Doctor, I just came to ask you for some pain killers for my father. His arm hurts him sometimes as he cannot straighten it anymore. But we gave him a course of vitamin injections and look how much stronger he is. They have made a real difference."

"Vitamin injections have done nothing!" I wanted to scream, "His persistence in going for a walk every day has done a whole lot. Why do they spend their money on buying these injections instead of cooking him some wholesome soups?" There seemed to be no way of convincing them. I knew I needed patience. Their lack of education and ignorance was blinding them to what might really help their situation.

Gradually we became busier attending in the village, as people grew in confidence in us and more people came to see us. Mothers brought their children for parasite medicines, coughs and colds. Older people came for treatment of diabetes and high blood pressure. Women came for help with family planning and antenatal checks.

We had several regulars now. Felicita popped in bright and cheery for her diabetic check and medicines, and Janet brought Victor from the orphanage with nappy rash. Monserrat made a great fuss of him, which he responded to with his customary smiles and giggles. Aida came in with her cousin to proudly purchase her anti-epileptic medication. They were very happy at how much less frequent the attacks were already, and continued to bring me purses to sell regularly.

But in the evenings, when I was home alone, I continued to battle with loneliness, missing my friends and family back in the UK.

The day of my thirtieth birthday I was on duty in the Paediatric department in town. I felt a little depressed. The morning had been the usual collection of coughs, diarrhoea and worms, along with the inevitable frustrations of the lack of medicines to give out to these sick children. To make matters worse a group of loud, coarse speaking women had arrived just before the lunch hour rudely demanding I attend their children then and there despite not having any appointments.

"Doctor, don't be a bad person," they shouted, "The awful woman at reception would not give us any appointments for today, and our children need to be seen immediately."

I looked at the motley crew of snotty noses and dirty faces, and thought to myself that while they probably did need medical attention it hardly looked as though any of them were emergency cases. As for asking me not to be bad, that really got on my nerves. What was I doing here in a foreign land, giving them my time and expertise for free if I were a bad person for goodness sake? My suggestion that they wait until I returned from my lunch break for me to attend them went down like a lead balloon. I certainly did not feel like Queen Elizabeth coping serenely with all circumstances. I had let the frustrations get to me and forgotten to try and put myself in their shoes.

Now I still had an hour to go until home time, and I was alone and bored. Turning thirty felt like a huge milestone. I could hear my biological clock ticking – loudly – and there was nothing I could do about it. At lunchtime I had picked up an email from my brother, proudly announcing his engagement to a beautiful girl he had met on an internet singles site. "Maybe I should give it a go", I thought. But what on earth could I write in my advert? "Good looking, intelligent thirty year old looking for handsome, witty professional willing to up sticks and travel to Ecuador for the next few years." It just wasn't going to happen, I told myself despondently.

"Am I in my right mind being here?" I asked myself. "How long am I realistically going to stick this out? It is all very well, this thinking God wants me to doctor the poor and needy here in Ecuador, but it is pretty lonely out here all by myself. People here view life from such a different perspective; no one has a clue what kind of life I lived before, or thinks like I do. No one can really connect with me at a deep level or converse about things that really matter to me. I do want to follow God no matter what, to follow His calling and to love these dear people, but to be honest I would also love to have a family: some little girls to look after and bring up, to create memories with and to share cuddles with over bedtime stories. Why can't I give this desire up into God's hands?"

I decided to go home and spend the evening watching DVDs of All Creatures Great and Small, to wallow in nostalgia watching the crisp green pastures of home, and nurse my fit of homesickness. But when I arrived at my gate I found the health promoters had all got together to organise a party for me at Mary's house. What a lovely surprise.

We had a great time, eating the fried chicken and chips they had prepared, playing silly games and falling about in laughter. There was even a cake, with candles to be blown out, and wishes to be made. It ended up a special, friend-filled evening, one of those never to be forgotten evenings that surprise you with the love and companionship they contain. I went to bed feeling appreciated, a smile on my face. It was as if God had reached down and given me a hug of encouragement. I was ready to embrace another day in Ecuador.

## CHAPTER SEVEN

# White Roses

God soon brought more people needing help my way. The next day in town a four year old boy, Jose, was brought to see me by a local Christian Charity, Life in Abundance Trust. "How can I help you?" I asked his very young looking mother.

Looking very anxious she began, "Jose had an eye removed soon after birth due to cancer of the retina, and now he is blind in the other. I don't know what to do. I have six children – my baby is only three months old – and my husband drinks all his money away. He does not help me provide for the children at all, and I don't know how I can afford to find a doctor for Jose."

"Have you not been back for follow up appointments after his operation as a baby?" I enquired. She shook her head rather shame faced. "I could never afford the bus fares to Quito, Doctorita. They did tell me to take him back but I just couldn't."

"We want to help this little boy, Doctorita. But we don't know what treatment he needs. What do you recommend?" The Charity worker chipped in.

"He needs to go and see the eye specialist in Quito urgently," I replied, very concerned for the disfigured little boy quietly seated before me on his mother's knee. I was determined to pull out all the stops to help this precious little boy. "Let me make some phone calls and see what we can arrange."

I soon found myself on the bus to Quito with Jose and his Mum. Jose behaved himself perfectly, listening intently to all that went on around him to compensate for his lack of sight. He allowed the specialist to examine his eyes, and patiently underwent various tests as the day went on. I spent the day making repeated trips to the cashier to pay for each test that was ordered. The whole experience was so different from the free-at-point-of-use NHS.

We spent the night in a hostel, and the following day the doctor broke the news to us that Jose had the cancer in the other eye and needed an operation that would cost eight hundred dollars.

Jose's mother's face fell. There was no way she would be able to pay. I was also thinking through the implications. It was a large amount of money that would stretch the charity's resources. The same sum could build toilets for eight families in the village, or pay for six children to attend school that year. What was more important? How should I make such decisions? At the end of the day I knew that we had that amount in the bank at that time, and that this uncomplaining little boy needed help. So I paid up and left Jose at the hospital for his operation.

I had a request to help another cancer patient with palliative care. This time it was a woman aged forty, Celia, who had advanced breast cancer. I went to visit her with Monserrat, and met her husband and nine year old son. They were so relieved to have someone visit to help their loved one. They were abandoned and distressed. It was as if the angels had guided us to their side.

Monserrat peeled off the dressings to reveal a huge, bleeding, smelly tumour covering all Celia's chest and half her back. Monserrat looked at me in horror, as we asked who was doing the dressing changes.

"I am," responded Celia's sister-in-law in tears, "but I don't really know how to. The wound weeps all the time and smells awful. Can you help me?"

Monserrat set to cleaning the terrible tumour gently, and explained how to dress it so that it would not smell. I continued to examine Celia. She was in terrible pain, had grossly swollen legs and difficulty breathing.

I wanted to give her some morphine, but getting hold of some was the challenge. I explained the problem to Celia's family. "Morphine would be really useful to control Celia's pain and also to help her breathing, but there simply isn't any here in Santo Domingo. We need someone to be able to go to Quito to the Jersey Foundation to obtain some. Is there someone who could go?"

"Of course," stated her brother, willing to drop everything at a moment's notice. "I will go tomorrow. Just explain to me what I have to do."

"Excellent," I breathed a sigh of relief, "it will make all the difference to Celia. Let me show you how to position Celia to help relieve the breathlessness meantime, and we can lend you some soft cushions and a special mattress to help prevent pressure sores."

As we drove home Monserrat and I sat in stunned silence. I had never seen anything like that tumour before. It had repulsed me. It broke my heart thinking of that young mother no longer able to bring up her dearly loved little boy. There did not seem to be words to express our sentiments, so we parted with a heart-felt hug, planning to return and visit that family again soon.

My heart rebelled at the whole tragic situation. "Why do these awful things happen to such lovely, uncomplaining people?" I raged at God, "She is such a young woman still. She has a young family. Why is she suffering so, and facing imminent death, when You have the power to heal her?" I did not understand God's ways, but I did believe that He loved Celia and her family, and I wanted to show them that love in all the ways I could. At least there were many things we could do to help them; make her pain and suffering less, comfort her family, assure them they were not facing this without support.

Our next visit to Celia was such a contrast. She was feeling relief from the pain and welcomed the visit of a Pastor. She found great comfort in having the Bible read to her and in the simple songs the Pastor sang to her accompanied by his somewhat battered guitar. As he gently sang "God is here, Alleluia," she knew it was true, and entrusted herself to His loving hands. The beautiful melodies wrought a peace around all of us who were gathered by her bedside, comforting and consoling.

Our visit ended with the offering of huge slices of watermelon. It was so sweet and juicy the juice literally ran off my chin as I guiltily tried to stop it dripping onto their one patch of carpet that covered the cement floor. I was so glad to be able to reduce their pain in some measure. I felt I was in the place I should be. I was neither superhuman, nor revered specialist, nor saint, but my simple willingness to live in this forgotten part of the world meant I could make the world a better place for some, and this gave me great joy.

I also felt that way when Jose's mother came to see me in the paediatric department. Jose was home, but she needed to take him back to Quito for a follow up appointment. She did not have the money for the bus fares. I could not imagine being in that situation: unable to do the simplest task for my child without the humiliation of having to ask for money. I went to meet them at the bus terminal early the next morning to buy their ticket, and to give them some fragrant freshly baked bread rolls to eat on the journey. I waved them off, these forgotten ones whose need God saw and remembered and was so glad to be able to give them a helping hand when they most needed it.

Sometimes I encountered the most unexpected situations and struggled to know how best to give that helping hand. As I drove up to Celia's house for her next visit I was alarmed to find all her extended family had arrived and were wailing hysterically outside her small room.

I could see her young son was in the midst of all the commotion very frightened and upset.

"What is going on?" Monserrat asked the nearest relative, who swallowed a sob to answer, "Celia is about to die. We have come in preparation for the wake. She is very bad."

I entered the room and asked all but the immediate family to leave so I could find out what had changed and how she needed her medications adjusted. Celia gladly hugged her son as best she could, and tried to reassure him. "I just felt breathless during the night, and it frightened the family." She explained. "But I am OK, really I am," she protested.

After we dressed her tumour and finished examining her, we just sat with Celia, her husband and son for a while, giving them time to be quiet together, removed from the chaos outside. Peace permeated the room once again. Maybe all this caterwauling was normal behaviour here, I wondered to myself, but it all seemed very high drama to me. I was not sure how I should respond. So we prayed with Celia, and hugged and reassured her son, and promised we would return again soon.

When I took my leave the extended family and friends outside clamoured to know how much more time Celia had left. I told them honestly only God knew that, but that she presently felt better than she had the day before. I beat a hasty retreat to my car most uncomfortable in pursuing this conversation any further.

Jose's Mum turned up again, this time to tell me that he had a broken arm. The doctor had told them he had tumour in the bone. My heart sank. The tumour had spread. There was now little hope for Jose.

I visited Jose at home now he was too unwell to go out. The family lived in a small cane house, with plastic sheeting forming the roof. I was pleasantly surprised to find it was spotlessly clean, despite the mud floor, and that they had cut plastic bottles to make plant pots for the brightly coloured flowers that adorned the outside.

I helped Jose with pain medications and we supported his Mum as best we could as she dedicated herself to looking after her little boy. His fragile body lay peacefully sleeping on the only mattress in the house, his pain well controlled. He was now mostly sleeping and just occasionally waking to drink a little soup. She welcomed the Pastor who accompanied me on that visit and his spiritual support as she struggled to come to terms with the gravity of her son's illness. When I left the house it was a scene of peace and tranquillity despite the unfolding tragedy within.

Suddenly I received a panicky phone call from Jose's mother, "The children's father arrived drunk last night and took all my children away, even the little baby I am still breast feeding." She hysterically wept. "He is now threatening to come and take Jose away from me as well. I am on my way to a relative's house. How could he do this to us? I just wanted my son to be able to die in peace."

I felt utterly inadequate and out of my depth. What could be done now? What was that father thinking in doing such a thing? Who could we appeal to, to defend her and her children? My heart bled for Jose, forced to make a long journey in his delicate state.

He died a few hours later, far from home and those who loved him.

I attended the funeral in the Catholic Church near his home, and then accompanied them to the burial in the grave yard built on top of an abandoned rubbish tip. Jose's brothers and sisters were still being held by their father and were unable to attend. While some local boys shovelled the earth in on top of the heartbreakingly small coffin Jose's mother fell to the ground sobbing great body-shaking sobs, and tried to throw herself into the grave. She had fought all she could, and lost. She was devastated and despairing. As her mother restrained her the neighbours put single white roses all over the mound of dirt. That image haunted my dreams for many days to come.

Later, Life in Abundance Trust workers helped her go to the authorities to get her other children back. They gave her the determination to carry on despite the tragedies life had dealt her. They gave her hope as they continued to share the love of Jesus with her.

I knew children died all over the world every day. I knew we lived in a sinful, selfish world. Jose's death still impacted me greatly; that little boy who had never had the chance to ride a bike or race around with his mates in the playground. The injustice of the whole scenario grieved my heart. But I believed it grieved Jesus heart too. I could not put wrong things right, but I could try and do what was right and good myself. I closed my eyes and pictured Jose with sparkling new eyes, gazing at Jesus, lost in his loving embrace. All was now well with Jose, his tears had been wiped away. It was time for me to continue to do what I could for those living around me.

The next day Monserrat and I went to visit Celia and found she was now unconscious. Her husband and son sat quietly beside her. She was relaxed, and not distressed. The rest of the family had not yet been called to come. She slipped away in the night and her family were so thankful she had had a peaceful death in the end.

"We want to thank you so much Monserrat for all your help in dressing Celia's tumour and you Doctorita for helping us take care of her. We had no one to turn to, and then you came along. It was such a relief to know how best to care for her in her last days, to have someone to call on. Thank you both." Celia's husband shook our hands warmly as we took our leave.

As I sat in Mary's kitchen drinking a cup of tea later that day, we quietly reflected on recent events. "I hope Celia's son will be alright," I said, "he is so young to have lost his mother."

"It is so sad," agreed Mary, "but I am sure his father and extended family will take good care of him. They seem a good family. How are you coping with things?"

"Oh I am OK," I assured her. "It helps to have a friend like you to share a cup of tea and a chat with. These situations are so tragic, but it is to be able to help people like Celia and Jose that I am here in Ecuador. It is what makes everything worthwhile. There seems to be no concept of palliative care here. When there are no more treatment options people are just sent home to die in pain. It is wonderful to be able to make them more comfortable, and offer them spiritual and emotional support as well. I think this is an area where there is a great need. It is such a privilege to be God's hands for these people."

Mary gave me a quick hug as I left to go back home for the night.

The second of November was a bank holiday for the Day of the Dead. The health centre was shut. I was free and curious to see what it was all about. I tagged along with the Orphaids children as they trouped up the road to the cemetery to visit the graves of their parents. Each grave was recently cleaned and painted, and families were gathering there to lay elaborate flower arrangements and food. There was an air of hushed solemnity while the people thronged whispering in quiet tones. Neighbours greeted each other, and the Priest mingled reciting prayers. I took a moment to stand and remember Jose and Celia; to celebrate their bravery and to pray for their loved ones who missed them.

Vladimir came up to greet me. "Do you celebrate this day in England?" he asked. "No," I responded, "I have never seen anything like this before."

"Then you won't have tasted Colada Morada either?" he suggested.

"What is that?" I enquired, interested.

"Come over here and try some," he directed. It was a sweet juice made of red berries and herbs, and was quite delicious. Vladimir also purchased a bread roll shaped like a child and decorated with colourful icing for me to try. "These are the traditional rolls to eat with the juice," he informed me, anxious to introduce me to the complete Day of the Dead experience. "Do you like it?"

"Yes," I smiled, "it's nice of you to take the time to show me. Thanks." He gave me a friendly hug as he turned to go, sensing my contemplative mood. I was grateful for the human touch.

After taking my leave I ran to catch up the Orphaids children who were now setting off for home. A glance over my shoulder revealed Vladimir still staring wistfully after me. I played with the children in the garden until sunset, their laughter and fun reminding me that life triumphed over death. Victor sat watching the other children chasing each other, joining in with their laughter from his pushchair. He seemed to be taller every time I saw him, growing stronger every day, despite the illnesses he battled with.

"What a mixture life is here," I mused, "There is such suffering, and so many opportunities to give a helping hand. There are those who help themselves tremendously and those who seem to be sinking in a quagmire of ignorance and vices. It seems like every day I go from feeling appreciated to feeling frustrated, from sharing in the most intimate moments to feeling utterly alone, from moments of pure joy to moments of terrible tragedy. God brings me through it all; moment by moment He is with me. May I be faithful in serving Him."

## CHAPTER EIGHT

# The Wonders of Donkey Fat

I watched the news incredulously as they recounted the story of a child healer who had come to Ecuador, who was reported to work miracles. Thousands upon thousands of Ecuadoreans flocked to be touched by this child. They went in their wheelchairs, and leaning on sticks, hoping for a cure for their diabetes, AIDS or cancer. Why did so many people believe in this child? I wondered.

I was still struggling to convince people to trust me enough to take my advice. "It is so frustrating after studying all those years in a world class University that people here do not believe I know what I am talking about," I complained to the ever ready to listen Mary. "A woman came with her husband the other day. He had a cold, so I gave him some paracetamol and decongestant medicines to help his symptoms and reassured him that he would get better in a few days time. After twenty four hours he still had a cold so he went to a pharmacy, where they gave him a single shot of penicillin, and then, due to the natural course of a cold, he started feeling better. Today I bumped into his wife who shook her head sadly and said my tablets did no good at all and that she had had to take her husband for an injection. "You should use an injection next time doctor," she recommended "See what good it did my husband!" People here do not give treatments time to work. They expect miracles."

Mary laughed, "That's just the way it is here. And people love to offer advice on any and all occasions. If Liliana has a wound on her finger the child next door will tell her to put leaves on it, her Auntie will tell her to use an antibiotic cream that helped her once, and a complete stranger in the queue for the bus will tell her to get an injection of vitamins to cleanse her blood so it does not get infected. Liliana will believe all of them, and try out all their suggestions."

I chuckled at this accurate picture. "People never ask themselves what qualifies the person giving them advice to be able to recommend a remedy. Everyone quotes anecdotal evidence as the gospel truth. No one has heard of double blind randomised controlled trials. I suppose it comes down to the lack of education. No one has been taught how to evaluate what they hear."

"It causes all kinds of problems," agreed Mary, "The other day a worker of ours had some stomach cramps. His mother had been given some medication once, for what she thought had been a similar complaint, so she gave some to him to take. They did not know what the correct dose was, so he took an overdose, and the medication also interacted with his blood pressure tablets, so he ended up in the emergency department of the hospital. Lots of your patients will have self-medicated before they come to see you."

"And they don't only take medicines!" I exclaimed. "I had a patient this week that was dying of gastric cancer. Her family had fed her vulture blood and paid hundreds of dollars for natural remedies their sellers promised would cure the cancer. Her distraught husband asked me if I thought the putrefied snake preserved in neat alcohol a friend had given him might save her." Mary grimaced at the thought. "Her family were simply desperate to save her, and believed anyone who offered them hope."

"People are very superstitious here." Mary explained. "Our neighbour, an elderly lady, told me that a man came to see her, claiming to be a witchdoctor. He told her that someone in her family was destined to die very soon. Then he informed her that if she gave him her best chickens he would make sure it did not happen. She was genuinely afraid and gave him the chickens."

"Maybe I should scare people into taking my medicines," I joked, "Or take to injecting vitamins to cure all ills. Do you know I realised this week that the most popular vitamin injection also comes in a version that includes Diclofenac, so it will actually relieve your pain. The drug company just charges you twenty times more than the same generic Diclofenac injection would cost you."

"People are defenceless against these scams." Mary commented. "They do not know any better."

Wandering home that afternoon Vladimir caught up with me and we got into conversation. "People are very ingenious here," I commented, wondering what Vladimir made of the local old wives tales and practices. "A man cut himself today with his machete and he put some burnt herbs on the cut to stop the bleeding. They seemed to have done the trick, but they were very difficult to clean off to be able to stitch the wound. Sometimes patients come with the thin white membrane found just inside the shell of a boiled egg closing a wound. It actually works like butterfly stitches or a plaster."

"There is a tree called dragon-blood in our garden which comes from the jungle. The sap of the tree is used as an antiseptic for wounds. Have you seen it?" Vladimir asked.

"I have seen people bathing wounds in boiled up herbs of various descriptions," I replied. "I have also seen people put frogs on infected skin. Why they think a frog is going to stop pus oozing from their legs I don't know!"

"The older folk have all kinds of old wives tales." Vladimir agreed with a half-smile.

"Not just the older people," I continued emphatically, "a well-educated, wealthy mother told me in no uncertain terms she did not want to try inhalers for her daughter who has asthma as she was of the opinion the maggots and donkey fat she was feeding her daughter would cure her, whereas she understood inhalers were only to control the symptoms."

"Oh that is a common remedy from Loja, at the south of Ecuador, where they eat donkeys. My father gave me donkey fat when I was little and claims it cured my asthma." Vladimir laughed.

"There are lots of natural remedies that may have some value," I conceded. "People drink Aloe Vera for gastritis, and apply it to their hair and skin to make it fresh and shiny looking. I'm not so sure about eating snakes for medicinal purposes."

"My Aunt swears by a mixture of tree tomato and cucumber juice to lower cholesterol. The tree tomato has to be liquidised skin and all, which makes it a very bitter concoction, but many people are convinced that it works. You should do a study on it." Vladimir told me.

"Chamomile is a favourite herb here," I reflected, "It is used for bathing babies, inhaling for colds, or for washing infected eyes and skin. Eucalyptus is also boiled up for inhalation as a decongestant. Papaya seeds are used as a natural remedy for constipation and intestinal worms aren't they? Oregano and aniseed are given to babies to bring up wind. Leaves from the Obo tree are used for bathing babies to prevent nappy rash. There are lots of remedies I could study." I laughed.

"My Mum takes a remedy for gall bladder stones every year." Vladimir told me. "I would love to know if that really works or not. She drinks this green drink followed by a bottle of olive oil, then collects these rock hard stones that come out in her stools, and is convinced that they are gall bladder stones. Do you think they are?"

"I shouldn't think so," I shook my head, "But you could always take them to a laboratory to find out."

We were arriving at the gate of the orphanage, so I turned to go. "It has been fascinating talking to you," Vladimir told me, "Now make sure you eat some cat's claws before bed so that you never get cancer."

"I'll bear that in mind" I joked as Vladimir gave me a kiss good bye and I slipped inside the gate. I walked jauntily up to my house. It was stimulating to find someone to hold an interesting conversation with.

I now felt that each day was an adventure, with some new gem of knowledge to discover, or crazy custom to wonder at. It was definitely never boring. Gradually some people chose to believe in me and my Western style of medicine. A patient returned to be seen for a second time, as she felt better after taking the medicines I had given her the first time. What a victory! A man came after his neighbour told him I had cured his illness. What a recommendation! A woman came to bring me some eggs as a thank you for helping her sick child. What an encouragement to be so appreciated! Little by little I was able to help those around me more and more. I looked for ways to be of help to those around me.

The next day I decided to go and visit Alicia and Jeovhanny. I had not forgotten my concern that the girls were not going to school. Driving up the track to their village I enjoyed the view of the hills in the distance, and the pigs, cows, chickens and horses that wandered alongside the road. Jeovhanny was sitting up in bed bright and cheerful, and Alicia was keen to show me how their plants were coming along. As I walked through the flower beds I marvelled at the beautiful rich pink colour in the blooms.

"How are your girls?" I asked them.

"They are well, thank you." They replied.

"Are they going to school?" I enquired. Jeovhanny and Alicia exchanged glances nervously. "Well, Maricela is," they replied. "She walks an hour each day to get to the secondary school. But we need one of the girls here in the house to help with Jeovhanny, so Gabriela is not able to go as well."

"Have you considered sending her to a school that gives classes at the weekend in town?" I asked them. I had been doing a bit of homework before coming to see them, and was armed with suggestions. "That way she could go as well."

"Hmm, we had not thought of that," they conceded. "But how much would it cost?"

"Why don't we look into it." I suggested. "You find out the cost and I will see if I can find a sponsor for her. You never know, there may be someone willing to help her study."

"That would be amazing!" They exclaimed. "We do feel badly that we are not giving both of them the chance to study."

I made my way home to send some emails. I felt energized and excited when I found solutions to seemingly insurmountable obstacles in people's lives. It made being in Ecuador worthwhile. The gift of an education was the gift of a job, a career, the means to provide for her family and the knowledge of how better to care for them. It was the gift of self-confidence, achievement and taking one's place in the world. I thanked God for the opportunity to give this gift to bright Gabriela who sacrificed her youth to care for her sick father.

I also had the chance to help an old man in the village who decided to trust us to treat him. Monserrat's father, Oswaldo decided to come to the village health centre for his treatment when he became unwell with a lung disease. He came regularly for many months, stating, "May God grant you wisdom as you treat me, Doctorita," each time he arrived. He was such a pleasant man, always ready with a friendly greeting, and a favourite with the young people of the village. Gradually his health declined and he was less and less able to get out and about to watch the youngsters playing football as he had before. Still he walked, ever slower to the health centre for his check ups, so grateful for the help he received, even though it was becoming obvious he was not going to recover. I felt honoured that he had chosen to put his trust in me as his doctor and did all I could to help him.

I also wondered a little anxiously what people might think when I lost a patient. Would it destroy the fragile trust that was developing with the villagers? Would they mutter and say he should have gone elsewhere for treatment? Or would they be accepting that some illnesses had no cure.

It was late afternoon when I arrived back from work in the health centre in town to find Monserrat waiting for me at my house, wanting me to go and see her father. "Please come quickly Doctorita. My father is in great pain. He has gone to bed and cannot move his leg. It is all white and cold."

I was immediately alarmed and hurried with her to see Oswaldo. Looking at his leg my heart sank to see it was without circulation. "Quick," I instructed, "Let's get him into my car and take him to the hospital. This is an emergency."

The emergency department was jammed full of people needing help. It was desperately understaffed and under equipped. Patients were lying around on trolleys and in wheelchairs crying out in pain, waiting for someone to attend to them.

The doctor on duty explained to us that there was no vascular specialist in Santo Domingo, so the only hope was to go to Quito, three hours' drive up the windy mountain road. Those of us accompanying the family had a whip round to find the cash needed for the ambulance, and I held his hand as he lay on the hospital trolley waiting for arrangements to be made.

"Please pray for me," Oswaldo whispered to me, suspecting that his time was now short. "And may God repay you for all you have done to help me." Tears filled my eyes. I had been able to do so little to help him in reality. I held his hand all the firmer and prayed as he asked, giving thanks for his life and putting him into God's hands. Humanly speaking his chances of survival were decreasing with each minute that passed without him being near the specialist help he so desperately needed. I believe that for all of us ultimately our times are in God's hands, and I felt a sense of privilege at being the person who could accompany Oswaldo in those moments as he prepared to meet his Maker. But I also felt sad and angry that this man, dearly loved to his family and equally as important as any other human being, did not have the same opportunity for life saving treatment as others would have had in a different place and time.

A few hours later Oswaldo set off up the mountains to the capital city with its specialists and technology. Tragically, predictably, it was all too late. Gangrene set in and he died the following day.

When I arrived at the wake I greeted the many villagers sitting outside Oswaldo's house. I felt sad at all that had happened and also wondered what his family thought of me and my doctoring skills now.

Monserrat and her mother both came out of the house to greet me.

"I am so sorry there was not more I could do," I began as we shed tears together.

"No, no, Doctorita, we know you did all that could be done. This was his destiny. It was God's will. We are very grateful to you for all your help. You looked after him well for many months. He was very happy to have you for his doctor. He never wanted us to take him elsewhere. It was just time for God to take him. Come and take a seat here with us. Accompany us a while." I was grateful for their kind words, though the sadness I felt at losing a patient remained.

Later, before I left, I took a last look at Oswaldo's now still, pale face in the open coffin, and bid farewell to a brave and well-loved neighbour, father and grandfather, silently apologising to him that I had not been able to do more to save him. He would be sorely missed.

"People just accept there is nothing more that can be done here, don't they?" I commented to Mary. "I cannot help comparing the lack of facilities here with the air ambulances in Scotland, ready to take patients from remote areas quickly to the specialists they require."

"People here do not know any different," Mary explained. "They live within the realms of what is possible here in Santo Domingo. Oswaldo's family will mourn their loss of course, but they will then turn their energies to living the life remaining to them the best they know how."

There was something healthy in this attitude to life. The funeral completed, the talk of the village was the hunting of some armadillos. Monserrat was in the middle of the group of women who set to barbequing the animals for all to enjoy. I felt honoured to be invited to try some. Monserrat chose what she thought looked one of the finer cuts and put it on a plate for me along with some boiled manioc, salad and rice. I gingerly bit into the meat while everyone else looked at me with baited breath in eager anticipation of my reaction to this delicacy. Actually I was pleasantly surprised - the meat was delicious. Everyone smiled and relaxed at this pronouncement, and the general chatter carried on once more. It was good to see that life did indeed go on. I felt that the villagers were beginning to get to know me and trust me in some measure. They were opening their hearts and giving me the chance to show them the love God longed to shower them with. It was time to relax and enjoy the ride.

## CHAPTER NINE

# A Little Princess

Christmas arrived, and I was looking forward to sharing the festive season with the villagers and joining in their celebrations. It was certainly going to be different to making snowmen and pulling crackers, eating mince pies and singing Christmas carols, while swathed in thick woolly jumpers to keep warm.

Santo Domingo was starting to heat up as the rainy season approached. Temperatures were between thirty and forty degrees, as the sun blazed down during the day scorching everyone in sight. In the afternoons, around three o'clock, the sky would suddenly darken ominously and everyone grabbed their washing in off the lines and ran for cover. Tremendous downpours of rain erupted from the heavens, accompanied by forked lightening and deafening claps of thunder, causing frequent power cuts and flash floods.

Families put up brightly coloured tinsel and made nativity scenes. There was a life size one in the town square, with models of Mary and Joseph and baby Jesus in the manger, and straw strewn around the ground.

In people's homes they had smaller versions, with little china figures and toy animals, set in some grass and flowers brought in from the garden. I liked this custom, this visual reminder wherever you turned, of the real meaning of Christmas.

Many villagers were too poor to be able to afford Christmas presents for their children. The traditional gift was a bag of biscuits and sweets given to each child at their school. I was asked to donate twenty bags of sweets to the local school. I consulted Monserrat as to what these bags should contain, and then gladly set about filling them.

Having duly handed in the bags of sweets to the school teacher I was invited to the school Christmas programme. This took place the afternoon of the twenty fourth of December, Noche Buena, "the good night".

The children played some games; youngsters tried to climb a greasy pole to reach the prize carefully tied to the top, others jumped in sack races and ran three legged races. Then they had a singing competition with the children queuing up to sing a Christmas song into the microphone of the compeer, anxious to win a prize. It was a source of great hilarity and applause. Then the smallest girls in the school dressed up in lacy, frilly dresses, with elaborately arranged hair, and paraded up and down a cat walk. I was asked to be one of the judges to choose the Little Christmas Princess. Each little five year old girl had to introduce herself, then model up and down, hands on hips, turning round and round to show off her costume. There were five judges. We each gave a mark out of ten to each small girl, then the totals were added up and the winner announced. It was so hard to choose between them – they were so cute and so brave to stand up in front of the rest of the school and all the parents gathered for the event. When Paola heard she had won she blushed and curtsied and stepped forward to receive her crown and sash embroidered with the word "Princess". She also received a toy that had been donated for the winner. The runners up were then given sashes that proclaimed them "Little Star" and "Little Fairy" to wear across their chests, and were given gifts as well. All the girls were delighted with their toys, and ran off for a hug from their proud Mums.

The Mums had cooked a vast quantity of Colorado Rice so that every child would receive a plateful. This was a typical local risotto, made with rice, chicken, carrots, peas, onion, chorizo sausage and coloured yellow with the achiote bean. It made me laugh to see the children jostle and fight to get a plateful, and then cheekily try for seconds claiming it was for their old granny.

Finally there was great excitement as first the children and then the adults lined up to receive their bag of sweets. The only present many of them would receive that year, they were made very happy by this simple gift. As I watched, and was then given my bag, I determined to raise some funds the next year to be able to give the children a toy as well. What smiles it would bring to their faces were they all to receive such an unheard of luxury!

As the party broke up and families and neighbours set off along the road back home in the dusk, the dark clouds now gathering ominously overhead, those who could afford it would be celebrating with a Christmas meal that evening. Then any personal gifts might be exchanged as well, or the following day, the twenty fifth, some families would go into town, where all the shops were open on one of the busiest trading days of the year, and buy clothes or shoes for each other.

The orphans were taken on mass to buy a new pair of jeans for their present. They were buzzing with excitement as they left the orphanage, all piled into the back of the pick-up. Victor was riding up front and grinned at me out of the window as they went by. He might not have understood what was going on, but he always enjoyed an outing.

I spent Christmas Day at Mary's with some other ex-patriots. Mary out did herself in cooking turkey and roast potatoes, and someone brought a Christmas pudding that had been sent to them. I made some crackers, with hats and jokes. We sat around after lunch, sweltering in the heat of the day, imagining what our families back home would be doing. Then we played Christmas Pictionary and charades into the evening, and even managed to warble some carols from memory.

My family, gathered together in Scotland 'phoned me on Christmas day, and despite the delay on the line we managed to wish each other Merry Christmas. They were about to go for an after dinner walk with the dog in the crisp snow outside, while I was sweating away thinking a trip to a swimming pool might be more the order of the day.

And then, Boxing day, I had to go back to work at the health centre in town, where they presented me with my Christmas gift, a bag of groceries including sugar, rice, tinned peaches and tuna. It was back to life as usual.

Well, things almost returned to normal, as there were still New Year celebrations to come. The streets now filled with people selling heads made of papier-mâché and painted to resemble politicians, cartoon characters, men and women. Some came complete with bodies, and others were just the heads so you could make a body using old clothes stuffed with newspaper at home.

These characters were called "monigotes". They sat outside shops and houses, adorning the streets. Vladimir organised a group of us to go into town to admire the display the evening of the thirty-first. My favourite was a huge Spiderman someone had made and hung from the wall in a spider's web. "Do you make these in Scotland?" Vladimir asked me. "No," I replied, "In Scotland people organise street parties or folk go from house to house sharing tipples of whisky."

I was alarmed when a boy dressed up as a widow woman suddenly appeared at the car window begging for money. He had put on a frilly black blouse and black skirt with balloons for buttocks and bosom. Vladimir laughed at my startled expression. "It is another tradition here at New Year," he explained. "It is a great way for the youngsters to make a few dollars."

It was decided to have a "monigote" competition in the village that year. Several groups made a character together in a bid to win the prize of a jug of beer. Most of the villagers got together outside one of the shops to enjoy the fun, and the characters were put on display. All of the characters were made to resemble someone from the village; there was the president of the community, the school teacher and the organiser of the football team. There was one however that was instantly proclaimed the winner. One team had made their character look like the maintenance man of the village water system. They had really gone to town on it. He was complete with his glasses, his notebook and pen for taking the water readings, and sat on a wooden bicycle they had also made. Everyone laughed enjoying the striking resemblance and proclaimed them the winners.

At midnight the "monigotes" were burnt. The villagers gathered round the fires to watch all that hard work go to ashes. Vladimir told me the burning symbolised eradicating all the bad from the past year, giving a clean slate to go forward into the New Year. In all the surrounding villages and in the town families and neighbours were also setting alight their "monigotes", and the horizon glowed orange for a few minutes. On the hills around Santo Domingo fireworks were let off, and from the village we could see the bigger ones exploding in the night sky above us. Someone produced champagne, and tiny plastic cups were handed out containing a mouthful of it, ready for the New Year toast. The President of the community did the honours, and then everyone started hugging and kissing each other and wishing everyone all the very best for the year ahead.

Vladimir took his time over wishing me a Happy New Year, before moving on to greet the many members of his vast extended family who were present at the gathering. Many of the villagers stayed together drinking and dancing until the sun came up, then stumbled home to sleep most of the rest of New Years Day. Those who had gone to bed earlier took advantage of the day to have a trip to the river for a swim and barbeque with their families, making the most of the bank holiday, before going back to work or school on the second of January.

I relaxed in the hammock outside my house, listening to the buzzing, humming insects and reflected on the year gone by. It was a year I had spent in a foreign land, in which many of my dreams had come true. I had finally been able to start working legally as a doctor in Ecuador and was half way through the required government year. I was proud to now be fluent in Spanish, and pleased to be learning so much about the culture around me. I was so thankful for my privileged upbringing, supportive family back home, and for the plentiful resources at my fingertips. Daily I found myself filled with joy as I reached out to those in need. I thought of the patients I had been able to help; calming their pain, listening to their woes, or controlling their diseases. They made it worthwhile keeping going. It was for them that I was determined to stay.

There were downsides of course; hard days and dark moments, times when I wondered if I was not completely mad to be so far from my family and friends in a country so different to my own. I was challenged by the daily frustrations of life in Ecuador; the patience required to queue up and pay a bill, or to make contact with my family via the slow and unreliable internet café in town. I was learning to accept that it simply was not possible to achieve all that I expected to in a day because life was disorganised and inefficient and everything took ten times longer to do in Ecuador than it would have done in the UK. There were still times I felt like a child learning how to do the basic tasks in life all over again. Sometimes I felt like I was living in a different world altogether from that I had grown up in.

Yet on the other hand I did now feel strangely at home in this little village in Ecuador, and was growing to relax and enjoy the slower pace of life and the emphasis put on simply spending time with your fellow man. As the days went by I found God gave me the grace to accept the differences and even to embrace them. I was re-evaluating what was really important in life, and what my priorities and goals should be, and finding Ecuador offered some interesting answers to those questions.

I gazed up at the twinkling stars above me and looked to the year ahead wondering what new adventures lay in store for me. I also felt the solitude of having left behind my friends and wondered how they were celebrating the New Year. I wondered what companionship the coming months would contain, and day-dreamed this might just perhaps by some miracle be the year I met my Prince Charming – that special person to work beside me and raise a family with me. I prayed with all my heart that I would live the coming year in a manner that pleased my Heavenly Father who had blessed me with so much and that He would look upon me with joy.

## CHAPTER TEN

# The Building of a Dream

The year started with the exciting news that the community had the funds to buy half a hectare of land in the centre of the village on which we could build a community health centre. The loaned room in the orphanage had worked fine up until then, but it would be fantastic to have a community owned, purpose built health centre to continue the work in. The villagers would feel they owned the project more, having invested in it themselves. We would be working together for the good of all.

The purchase completed, we were then very grateful to hear that the mission Latin Link had agreed to send a team of eight university students to help build the health centre. They would not only provide their own labour for six weeks, but also funds to help buy the building materials.

The team flew into Quito, and Mary's husband Fred went to meet them in his pick-up truck to bring them down the mountains to the village. They thought it was a great adventure to do the spectacular journey through the Andean volcano chain bouncing along in the open back of the pick-up. In the village one of the women had prepared a house for them to use. The team arranged their sleeping mats, bags and mosquito nets in the two bedrooms within. They had an outside toilet and shower to use, and a gas stove to cook on. Other villagers had brought plates and cutlery for them to use, and some plastic chairs for them to sit on. They paid a local lady to wash their clothes by hand.

The village president kindly brought them some cooking bananas, but not knowing what they were some of the team started to eat them raw, wondering why they tasted a bit odd. It was time for some orientation to life in Ecuador.

First we warned them about being very careful with hygiene and food preparation in order to avoid getting the dreaded diarrhoea. Everything needed to be cooked, peeled or washed in a special disinfectant available for cleaning fruit and salads. We told them it was not a good idea to eat food sold on the street stalls as they would not have much resistance to the local bacteria. Flies abounded on the meat sold in the markets, and fruit and vegetables often had amoebas on them. We also warned them only to drink bottled or boiled water, never water from the tap.

Second they had to get used to being in a cash society. No longer could they wander into a store and pay by debit card. They had to take cash with them, and also be willing to bargain for the items they wished to buy. Inevitably seeing white people the prices asked would be double what an Ecuadorian would pay so they had to haggle to get a reasonable deal.

Next we scared them with stories of thefts in order to help them be careful with their belongings and avoid running into problems. We told them about the pickpockets who stole my purse on a bus, the mobile phone of a visitor on the tram in Quito, and the shock of unexpectedly feeling someone else's hand in your pocket. We warned them not to wear expensive jewellery to avoid earrings being ripped from their ears, as happened to a colleague walking the main street in Santo Domingo. I did not tell them about a taxi driver who had told me his finger had been cut off when someone stole his ring - I thought that might scare them too much.

We did tell them not to accept any pieces of paper from strangers in the street, as occasionally they contained a hypnotic drug. Once they had inhaled the powder victims would give away their bank details and have money stolen from them. A local pastor had recently been a victim, and had only been rescued from having his car stolen from him by a friend turning up and intervening at just the right moment.

We told them to keep their bags in front of them at all times when in town or on buses, as thieves slashed open back packs carried on people's backs to remove the contents.

We told them to keep their passports safely in the house, and to just carry a photocopy, as there was nothing worse that losing your papers. The hassle of getting new passports and visas did not even bear thinking about.

We took them for a tour into town, travelling on the rickety ranchera bus, and showed them the best spots to do their food shopping, use the internet, cash machines and the post office.

The team were upbeat and excited to be on this adventure. They were determined to make the most of their time in Ecuador, to enjoy working alongside the people of the village, and the inconveniences of life were all part of the experience.

They set to work on the foundations of the new health centre with great enthusiasm, impressing the local builders working alongside them no end.

I was still working in the health centre in town three days a week, treating the small children brought to me with their coughs and diarrhoea. More difficult to know how to help were the more complicated cases. A one year old girl was brought along with a big head. She had hydrocephaly; water accumulating in her brain. I passed a middle aged man on the street each morning that had never had his hydrocephaly corrected. His head was enormous, and he suffered from brain damage. I referred the little girl with this problem to the children's hospital in Quito, in the hopes they would be able to operate and correct the problem.

The parents came back again to tell me their neighbours had held a bingo event to raise funds for them. With this gift the parents had had the money to pay the fares to go to Quito and stay while their daughter was attended to. She received the help she needed due to her parents determination and her community's support. It was wonderful to see her healthy and happy and we thanked God she had received the help she needed.

Another baby was not so fortunate. She had a cleft palate. She was a tiny, tiny little person, as at three months old she still weighed her birth weight because her parents did not know how to feed her with this deformity. They had been to Quito to the children's hospital, but had been told the operation she needed would cost thousands of dollars. They gave up hope of being able to help their daughter despite all the advice they were given to take her back again. I saw them a couple of months later in the market where they had a stall, and they told me their little girl had died. How my heart grieved there had not been some way to help that tiny baby. She should have lived to run and play and laugh and learn. No one had fought for that precious child of God.

As I sat contemplating that tragic story there was a knock on the consulting room door. To my surprise Vladimir walked in.

"Hi," I greeted him, "What brings you here?"

"I came to bring you this ice-cream," he replied, handing me his gift.

"Why, thank you," I replied, somewhat bemused, "Have a seat."

"I was just having some blood tests done that my employer requires, so I thought I would pop in and say hello," he explained.

"So what have you been up to?" I asked, searching for something to say.

"I have just been buying my mother a washing machine." He replied. "She has washed by hand all her life, and that is hard work. I thought it was time she had some help. She is absolutely delighted. She just went off to buy some paint to paint the wall where she is going to put the washing machine to match."

"Wow that is so great you can help her like that." I responded impressed and tickled at the same time.

"No, it is the least I can do really. My parents made sure I studied secondary school and university, and that is why I have a good job now."

"Where do you work?" I asked him.

"On a chicken farm. I do the maintenance for the mechanical equipment. I have to keep the pumps running and then get the generators going whenever there is a power cut so that the chickens do not die."

"Do you like chickens?" I asked with a grin.

"I love tinkering with machines and electrics. I'm very glad to have a job I enjoy. What do you enjoy about your work?"

"In the village we have been helping a forty five year old woman who lives in one of the outlying hamlets. She has had ten children, two of whom have died. She came to us pregnant with another baby, and had high blood pressure. She is desperately poor, and could not afford any medicines. It was great to be able to help her with the medicines she needed, control her high blood pressure and see the birth of a healthy baby. That is the kind of work I enjoy doing."

The remainder of the afternoon passed rapidly and soon it was clocking out time. As Vladimir took his leave he warned me, "Now I know where you are you may well be seeing me again."

"It is always good to have some company once the day's patients have been attended to." I smiled, not adverse to companionship from this unexpected source.

The frustrations of life continued to bug me. On the way home I popped into the post office to find there was a huge parcel of bandages waiting for me sent by a kind nurse in the UK. The customs official examined the parcel and told me I would have to pay two hundred dollars in taxes for the bandages. "But, that is ridiculous," I protested," That is a lot more than the bandages are worth."

"But you see you should really go and get a permit in Quito to be able to receive medical goods. I am letting you have them without that document."

The thought of having to go to Quito and spend days on end chasing a permit sent shivers down my spine. I regretfully said, "I am afraid you will have to send them back. I can't afford that amount of money."

"One hundred and fifty then," he offered, obviously expecting to barter for the bribe he wanted to line his own pockets.

I shook my head sadly and turned to leave. I felt gutted my friend had gone to all the trouble of sending the bandages, only to have to send them back, but sometimes it seemed bureaucracy and corruption could not be beaten.

Having the team around those weeks helped me enormously to be able to cope with life's frustrations and tragedies. I could have a laugh and a joke with them in English, and their enthusiasm was a breath of fresh air which refreshed me after a difficult day's consultations and visits. It was entertaining to hear of their exploits and adventures, and such an encouragement to see our dream of a health centre for the village becoming reality. Sometimes I had to pinch myself to check it was all really happening, that it was not all a dream.

## CHAPTER ELEVEN

# A New Pair of Shoes

The team coped well with life in the village, so different from what they were used to back home. They got stuck in to digging holes, twisting iron, and sieving sand with gusto, working alongside the local builders. They compared their tans, won by hard work in the sun, and blistered fingers. They kept score of who suffered the most days of diarrhoea, and who had the most insect bites on their legs. The villagers were impressed by these young people who worked so hard, especially the girls who dug and mixed cement with the men.

The team worked the same hours as the villagers, from seven in the morning, until four in the afternoon, then showered off and jogged down to the football pitch to play with the boys. Football and volleyball were the usual sports of the village boys, but the team had also brought a rugby ball and cricket bat which they tried to teach to the locals, with some interesting results.

The children gravitated to the work site when they came out of school in the afternoons, and loved trying to chat to these giant white people who spoke little Spanish.

They were fascinated by these laughing visitors who always seemed to have time for them. The team did a great job of entertaining and befriending them, playing endless games and providing colouring sheets and crayons. They acted out Bible stories and sang simple songs. They giggled, joked and tickled, and received many hugs and smiles in return.

The children had no idea where England was, and no concept of where these tall, blonde strangers had appeared from. At best some of the older children thought England was somewhere in the USA. They could barely imagine what it would be like to fly in an aeroplane, or travel over the sea to a faraway land. They chuckled listening to the gringos gabbling away in English, wondering what the strange sounds meant, the more daring amongst them trying to pronounce some of the alien words they heard. The children imagined the families of the team members lived in mansions, like they had seen in movies, with Ferraris parked in the sweeping driveways. They thought all white people were incredibly rich and had unlimited resources.

The women of the village did not think the team were eating properly. Sandwiches did not qualify as a meal in their book. The team needed to eat more rice and chicken, or a good plate of beans and lentils to keep their strength up. They had never seen people simply boil up vegetables and eat them on a plate with meat and potatoes. Ecuadoreans usually only ate vegetables in soups. The villagers took the team gifts of local fruits; guavas, which were like giant bean pods with white cotton-wool like fruit inside containing a big black stone, and guanabanas, which were big green spiky balls with white flesh inside perfect for making delicious smoothies or milk shakes. They made them empanadas, with pastry made from green bananas, filled with cheese and deep fried.

One of the children the team befriended, Araceli, was having difficulty keeping up at school, so I decided to take her to town for an eye test. Esther, from the team, accompanied us, along with Araceli's little sister Kassandra. The small girls were very excited to have the luxurious experience of travelling to town in a car, and sat spell bound watching as we zoomed past the lush green banana plants on either side of the road. They had rarely been to town before, and when they had had the excitement of such a trip, it had been on the rickety ranchera. They could not wait to tell their school friends about this adventure.

Araceli and Kassandra lived in a dingy wooden shack, ate mostly green bananas and rice, and all their clothes were given to them second hand by kindly neighbours. Parking the car in the centre of town, we set off for the optician. On the way we bought them a pot of yoghurt each, of which they savoured every last spoonful. They did not eat yoghurt very often. In the optician they gasped at the sight of so many shiny spectacles and stared at the fish tank with its brightly coloured fish. The girls were fascinated: they had never seen anything like it before. Everything was new and different to them, a world of novelties waiting to be explored.

Araceli completed her eye test, unfazed by the strangeness of being made to sit in darkness and identify letters on the wall. She was discovered to be blind in her right eye. The ophthalmologist examined her and said the blindness had been caused by an untreated infection which had scarred the macula in her eye, permanently damaging her sight. There was nothing that could be done to help, except to take care of the remaining good eye and make sure Araceli had regular check ups. It did at least give a reason for her teacher to let her sit at the front of the class and have a little extra time to do her school work.

As we returned to the crowded streets of Santo Domingo to go back to the car Esther noticed that Kassandra was hobbling along because her shoes were too tight. "Oh that is horrible when your shoes pinch," Esther cried, "Let's go into this shoe shop. Here Kassandra, try on these shoes here. Do they fit better?" Kassandra nodded her head in wonder. Were these shoes really for her? "I am going to buy them for you." Esther answered her unvoiced question. The beam on Kassandra's face lasted for days, and she sought out Esther to give her thank you hugs every afternoon that remained of their visit.

The children loved having their photos taken; they posed for their picture to be taken, then ran to see the images on the digital cameras. They were enchanted by balloons, excited by bubbles and entranced by stickers. It was a summer they would never forget; the summer they played new games, learned to say "hello" and "thank you" in English, and received many trinkets. It was a summer of fun and friendship, of love and laughter shared across the continents. It was a summer of inspiration. It was a summer that reminded me of the summer I had first come to Ecuador, and it reminded me why I was still there.

Vladimir and his brother Frank made friends with the team and, proud of their country and its culture, were determined to give their new friends a real taste of Ecuador. They invited them to a barbeque restaurant in town, and made sure they all tasted the complete selection of meats on the grill. Once everyone was full one of the guys asked warily, "So what have we just eaten?"

With a wicked grin Vladimir answered, "Oh just some pork and beef, heart, kidney, liver and cow's udder." Esther turned a worrying shade of green, while Vladimir dissolved into fits of giggles at the expressions on their faces.

Concerned that the team were cooking English food for themselves, Vladimir and Frank went to the team's house to teach them how to fry bananas and cook manioc and whole fresh fish. They tried out their faltering English and taught them many useful phrases in Spanish. They invited them to swim in the river, and offered to cook them guinea pig.

Vladimir came to visit me again in the town health centre, this time just before my lunch break. "I noticed you are always reading books, so I bought you one to read in Spanish," he said, handing me a collection of inspirational short stories.

I was taken aback by this thoughtful gift. I had never seen an Ecuadorean reading a book. "Thanks very much," I replied, warmly, "that is really sweet of you."

"You are very welcome," he responded, and in a rush continued, "and I would like to invite you to come and eat in a great fish restaurant for lunch today."

I paused for a moment, thinking if I wanted to take this friendship further. I had never seriously considered dating an Ecuadorian: their reputation as deceitful womanisers had gone before them. But as I looked at his kind twinkling eyes, now preoccupied with what my response was going to be, I realised I did want to get to know him better. "Why not?" I answered, and off we went.

"This fish in coconut sauce is really delicious." I commented, really enjoying our meal.

"It is one of my favourites." Vladimir replied, "I love sea food. Have you tried ceviche?"

"I am afraid I usually cook English dishes," I confessed, "I don't know how to cook much Ecuadorean food."

"We are going to have to remedy that!" Vladimir exclaimed, enthusiastically, "There are loads of delicious dishes for you to try. Ceviche is a cold prawn soup made with lots of lime. It is divine. Encebollado is a tomato soup with fish and banana crisps. It makes a great breakfast. Guatita is traditional to Santo Domingo. It is made with stomach, cooked in peanut sauce: another of my favourites."

I could see that my initiation into Ecuadorean cuisine was about to begin.

The team worked so well together that they finished the foundations, supporting columns and roof of the health centre in record time. The flat cement roof had to be left to dry for two weeks before further building could proceed, so the team were rather disconcerted to have time on their hands, and asked what other work they could do to help the community. I immediately thought of those families who were still without a toilet, and asked if they would be willing to dig latrines. The team rose to the challenge magnificently. The team and the families involved were to provide the labour, and I had some charity funds to use to buy the materials. We were in business: no more pointless trips to the government sanitary department. I was so happy we could do something about the problem ourselves.

Araceli, her seven siblings and her parents who used the open fields as their toilet, Ilia, her elderly parents and daughter who had to use the neighbour's outhouse, Efrain, his pregnant wife and two small children who had no bathroom attached to their split bamboo shack, Pablo, his seven children and his wife, who had a smelly hole in the back garden, were all amongst those who benefited. The team split up into groups to go to the various houses needing help, and set to digging a deep hole. Darwin, the builder, went behind them constructing the cement lid for the hole, and placing the toilet bowl. The team helped lay the block walls for the outhouses, and tin roof. The families found some sacking or plastic sheeting to use as a door.

In this way we managed to give the twelve families most in need a toilet of their own, reducing their risk of infections and parasites. Gone were the smelly, fly-ridden open pit latrines, and in their place were clean, enclosed flushing toilets. We were all delighted with this fantastic achievement. The families were very grateful. They helped with the construction of their bathroom, and shared their food with the team. The team had a great attitude, willing to help in whatever way was needed, working with the local people with great affection, openness and determination. They radiated the love of God to those around them.

The team members took a day off and went on a visit to the Colorado Indians. These indigenous people of Santo Domingo had an open air museum where they demonstrated their thatched roof houses, their lances for hunting wild animals and their pet monkeys. They showed how the women wove the cloth for their skirts, and the way they constructed their fires to smoke their meat. They played their drums and bamboo xylophone, and pointed out plants they used for medicinal and ritual purposes. They spoke in Tsafaqui, their native language, and translated phrases into Spanish. They also had achiote berries on display, and showed how they crushed them and used them to paint their hair. The boys on the team thought that was great fun, and had a go at painting their own hair, faces and arms red. When they arrived back in the village Darwin, the young builder, fell about laughing at the sight of these crazy red headed foreigners. He was really enjoying working with them, and never ceased to be amused at the mad things they got up to.

All too soon the time came for the team to return home. They were leaving behind them a health centre well on the way to completion, families with hygienic toilets and children with memories of a summer filled with fun and laughter. They had touched many hearts through their practical demonstration of love and compassion. God's love was on view for all to see. There were many good byes to be said; the local lads challenged the visitors to a football match, and won, at which they whooped around the pitch with cries of victory. Vladimir and his family invited the team for a special meal one evening, sharing delicious food, silly jokes and photos for one last time. The health promoters cooked fried chicken and chips for the team's last lunch, which they ate outside the new health centre. They all grouped together for a photo shoot next to the construction, and asked the team to send them copies of the pictures.

Everyone gathered to wave the team off, as they hitched up their back packs ready for the journey home. There were tears and hugs all round, then the team piled into the pick-up and set off waving and laughing. I wandered off home, feeling a little sad at the goodbyes and panicky at the sight of the newly constructed health centre. Suddenly my house felt very empty and silent. The spectre of loneliness reared its ugly head again. But I could hardly just up and go home when so many people had dedicated so much time, money and effort to provide the means for me to stay. "Help," I thought, "How did this all come about anyway? What have I got myself into? You are going to have to help me here Father," I prayed, "Give me the inner strength to be able to stay and fulfil this mission I believe You have given me. Let me know You are with me in the hard moments."

Vladimir took me out for breakfast the next day. It was a great distraction. After breakfast he took me to a swimming resort which had many of the local animals on display. He made a great tour guide. His enthusiasm for the creatures rubbed off as he proudly showed them off. We saw guatusos and guantas, which were like giant rabbits, turtles and snakes, huge spiders, toucans and parrots, monkeys and tigrillos (a small wild cat). He bought me some sugar cane to try sucking on, and mouth-watering fresh fruit juices to drink. I had great fun swimming, laughing and joking with him. He made me feel very happy and made me forget my fears.

## CHAPTER TWELVE

# Merry-Go-Round

I was coming to the end of my year working in the town health centre, and could not believe how quickly the time had passed. At last I would be able to dedicate all my time to the people in the villages.

Felicita was still coming regularly for her diabetic checks, but I was now failing to control her diabetes sufficiently with the available medications. She needed to start on insulin. This presented several challenges, as not only could she not read numbers to be able to draw up the insulin, nor did she have a fridge to keep it in. "Wow," I thought, I have prescribed many things in my time, but I have never had to prescribe a 'fridge before!"

I bought them a small 'fridge from charity funds, and took it in the car to the end of the path that led to their house. Felicita's husband met me there. "Good day Doctorita," he greeted me. "Let me help you get this fine 'fridge to the house."

"It is rather heavy," I hesitated, not sure how we were going to manage to carry it across the two fields we had to cross to get to the house.

"No problem, Doctorita," he assured me, hoisting it high onto his back and setting off briskly as though it weighed nothing at all.

I hastily set off after him, amazed at how easy he made it look. Felicita greeted us at the house, and broke into a wide smile as the fridge was reverently placed on the rickety wooden table placed ready for it.

"Now Felicita, you need to learn how to inject the insulin," I began.

"I am going to help," spoke up her twelve year old son. "I know how to read numbers." He stated proudly.

So I showed him how to draw up the insulin and inject his mother, and how to check her blood sugars and note them down for me. He learnt quickly, proud to be able to help.

"How do these people survive?" I asked myself as I looked around the house, which really consisted of two rooms, a wooden bench to cook on and a few old hard wooden chairs. Mosquitoes buzzed freely in and out, even the chickens wandered through the house at will.

"Forgive us Doctorita, we have nothing to offer you," Felicita was embarrassed. "Please accept these eggs, and may God repay you for your kindness to us."

"You are welcome. May God bless you too." I replied as I took my leave and set off back to my car across the fields feeling on top of the world. It was good to be able to help those no one else was worrying about, and to make a real difference to their health and hence their ability to care for their families.

Enrique appeared at my house the next morning, "Good day Doctorita," he called, "We would be honoured if you would come to our wedding reception this evening."

"Thank you Enrique," I replied, "I would be honoured to come. Thank you for inviting me." I was genuinely pleased he and his bride Fredis, a patient of mine, had thought to include me, and was also interested to see what an Ecuadorean wedding would entail. I did have a chuckle about the last minute invitation. It was so typically Ecuadorean.

I turned up at the wedding reception to find all the guests sat around the garden on whatever they could find to perch on. "Welcome Doctorita," Fredis hurried to greet me and to make me welcome. "Come in and find a seat." I made my way round greeting the other guests, before finding a seat with Monserrat. Fredis and her family were serving the food, and they brought us plates brimming with fried pork, manioc and boiled maize.

After the food came the speeches, and these were done by the patrons of the wedding. They made a toast to the newly-weds with thimble-sized plastic cups of champagne, wishing them all the best. Lastly the cake was served, a light sponge covered in sweet cream and fruits.

Fredis and Enrique were dressed in their best clothes; no white gown or penguin suit. Their children were spruced up in their best clothes as well, and were having a great time enjoying the party, playing with their friends.

"In Scotland weddings take months to plan." I commented to Monserrat. "They cost thousands of dollars and cause huge amounts of stress. I like this wedding. It is simple, but it really feels like a family celebration with the support of the whole community."

"Weddings are usually quick here." Monserrat informed me. "After all, when you have decided to marry, why would you wait months to actually do it?"

"Us Brits like to plan everything well," I laughed. "Inviting people on the day of the wedding just would not work in Britain."

As I sat watching the dancing that followed I allowed myself to day-dream if this was where my friendship with Vladimir was heading. What would it be like to be married to an Ecuadorian? I wondered. It would be good to feel part of one of these huge, supportive extended families, who always looked out for each other. But it would mean compromises too; becoming accustomed to cooking Ecuadorean food and to different standards of living. Could we really understand each other? And what would it be like once children came along? Would the education offered here be adequate? Crumbs, I might end up staying here for ever and ever, until I was old and frail. Getting panicky, I was starting to get cold feet about the whole thing and decided a visit to Mary was in order.

"Do you know Vladimir and his family at all Mary?" I asked in what I hoped was a casual manner.

"Yes," replied Mary directly, refraining from asking the reason for my question in her typically respectful manner. "Vladimir helped us get our electricity connection for our house. He worked in the electric company at the time. He is always very helpful and friendly. I usually see him playing football with the boys or teasing the children in the village. He seems to always have time for the youngsters."

"He seems to have a lot of time for me at the moment," I hinted, "and I am starting to have a lot of time for him."

Mary smiled a girlish grin, her eyes twinkling. "His parents serve on the water committee for the village. I know them better. They worked very hard for the community when they were doing the water project. They are a nice family. I am happy for you."

"Oh help," I thought, "Maybe it isn't time to write him off just yet. But how will I know if he is Mr Right? I do so want to have a family of my own, but it suddenly seems so scary."

"Well, with the bank holiday coming up I expect I'll see some more of him. I'll let you know how we get on," I confided with a smile.

The festival marking the anniversary of Santo Domingo happened each year on the third of July, and everyone in town, including us working in the health centre, had a couple of days free. There were parades in the streets. Many of the secondary school students dressed up in their best uniforms and marched through the streets playing drums and lyres in their school bands. On the Sunday there was a horse parade. The horses pranced through the streets showing off their prowess and antics. There was also a cattle show, where the best cows of the various different breeds were on display and stalls were set up selling farm goods and plants. In the showground in town many stalls were set up with people selling their handicrafts. People came from different parts of the country to sell clothes, bags, jewellery and typical foods. There was plenty to go out and see with Vladimir.

In the centre of town a fair had arrived with many rides to be enjoyed. There were small roller coasters and merry-go-rounds for the children and bigger rides that tipped you upside down and dashed you from side to side for the adults. They all looked rather precarious to be honest, but I reasoned no one seemed to have come to any harm so far, so I accepted Vladimir's invitation to go on one. He was not really at his best on the rides: even the gentle Ferris wheel made him feel nauseous. However not wishing to lose face he gallantly accompanied me on the biggest roller coaster, the boat that tipped you upside down and a train that zoomed round a vertical circle taking you upside down multiple times. We refrained from trying out the pirate boat, that swung relentlessly from side to side, after we had to offer first aid to a young man who had been carried off it in a dead faint.

We wandered the grounds enjoying the bright lights and carnival atmosphere, munching on hamburgers and popcorn. We failed to win a prize on the rifle shooting stall, and rested sitting on the wall at the edge of the park. When in his company all my fears melted away, I wished we were never apart. I felt more alive, full of energy, and loved. It was a heady mix. Vladimir bought a red rose from a child, and presented it to me, winning his first kiss from the white girl he had been pursuing. It was an evening of fireworks and thrills, and I welcomed his embrace as he took me back home. I wished that the holiday would never end.

But all good things come to an end. Vladimir had to go back to work and I, having finished my year at the health centre in town, had to head to Quito again to obtain my full registration as a doctor in Ecuador.

I returned to earth with a bump as I faced the frustration of being sent for one document after another. I lost count of how many offices I visited, how many taxis I took, how many photocopies I had to make. I rode the bus to and from Quito, closing my eyes so as not to see the drivers overtaking on hairpin bends and the ever threatening precipice along the roadside.

"Have they given you your medical registration document yet?" the health promoters asked me every few days, and every time I replied, "No, not yet, but I must be getting close."

Every time I went to Quito thinking this would be it, this would be the time they gave me my certificate, there was some other document I had to go and request.

A colleague had noticed my growing friendship with Vladimir, though as yet it was not common knowledge. He took me aside and warned me about the dangers of forming a relationship with an Ecuadorian. "You need to be careful," he warned me, "Latin men are not like British ones. Lies and half-truths are normal here. He will tell you what he thinks you want to hear to win you over. Latin men are renowned for their infidelity. How do you know he does not have another girl where he is working? You don't have anything in common with him. He will distract you from your work for God; even take you away from your intimacy with your Lord. He is only after the prestige of having a white girlfriend and probably your money as well. Maybe he wants a passport to the UK. If you want to keep serving God here you need to give up this friendship. It is only going to end in heart-break and disaster. I have seen it all before."

It was a strong warning, and it did make me stop and think. How well did I really know Vladimir? Could I really trust him, or was it all a big conspiracy? Did he really love me, or was he just after my white skin? Was he helping me serve God in this place? Was he the man God had for me? Or was I just being blinded by my loneliness and desire for a family, taking what was never intended for my good?

Vladimir was far away working on the chicken farm, and in his absence the seeds of doubt planted in my mind grew. I wanted with all my heart to follow God, to do His will, and did not want to be pursuing a relationship that would lead me away from Him. "Father I want to live my life for You. I know You want the very best for me," I prayed with my whole heart. "I surrender my relationship with Vladimir, and place my future back in your hands."

I 'phoned Vladimir and told him that I did not think we had much in common, that I was not sure I was ready for a relationship with him, that I wanted to serve God with all my heart. As I ended the call the tears came, but I was determined to do what seemed to be right and to trust God for my future.

## CHAPTER THIRTEEN

# Sewing for Life

Young visitors started coming to my gate to ask for help. Tania was a twelve year old who had finished primary school and was not going to secondary school.

"Doctorita, I have come to ask you a big favour," she commenced with trepidation. "I want to go to secondary school, but my parents will not send me because they cannot afford the books and the bus fares. I heard that you help Aida by buying her sewing. I am a good sewer. Maybe if you could buy my work my parents would send me to school."

"Let's go and speak to them," I responded, and off we went down the road to her ramshackle house.

"Good day Señor, Señora," I began, "Tania came to see me because she wants to go to school. I understand that you do not have the resources to send her, but if I were to buy her sewing regularly, would you let her go?"

Tania waited with baited breath for their reply. Her father thought for a moment then pronounced, "I think it would be good for Tania to study because she has a fungal infection in her hands which means she cannot cook or wash the dishes. I am afraid she will never find a husband, so she should have an education to be able to provide for herself. If you are willing to help her economically I will send her to school."

As I looked at the beautiful young girl standing before us with her perfect ringlets and exquisite smile, I could not imagine for one moment she was destined to remain single. However, whatever their reasoning, her parents had agreed, so I accepted Tania into the sewing group and set her some goods to stitch. She turned out to be able to do the most delicate embroidery and glowed at the prospect of studying.

The next girl to come and visit me was Jenny. She had learnt to make jewellery in a class at school. The oldest of three sisters, her parents said they could not afford to send her to secondary school. Indeed her father commented he did not see the point of educating girls. Jenny was desperate to go. She did not want to be languishing at home, but wanted to study so she could learn to be a teacher. She came to show me some of the jewellery she had made, and asked if I would be willing to help her sell some to give her an income to go to school. By now my Mum was doing a regular trade in her local church café, and visiting other groups and churches to set out her stall, and so I agreed we could try selling jewellery for Jenny along with the sewn goods. She skipped happily back home bursting to share her news.

I had not anticipated this turn of events, starting a sewing project to help girls fund their education, but it brimmed with tantalizing possibilities and sparkled with hope. So many of the problems I observed around me were caused at root by ignorance and poverty. The remedy to these was education. It was wonderful to be able to have an influence in the lives of these young people who were just starting out, to be able to help lift them out of the spiral of poverty and ignorance, to help them take their place in the world with dignity and self-respect. It filled me with joy to see the girls' smiling faces as they tackled their studies with enthusiasm, determined to make the most of the opportunity they were being given. I prayed for them daily, that they might know their Heavenly Father's love and provision for them, and trust Him with their lives. When they gathered to bring me their sewing we shared Bible readings and conversed about what was happening in their lives. We forged bonds of friendship and faith.

Sharing the work with my Mum in this way, as she gladly gave her time and energy to sell the goods voluntarily, also made me feel closer to home. The world seemed that bit smaller. I felt my links with home were strengthened. I felt more supported and understood. I knew that as people heard about the work of the sewing they also prayed for the girls and for me.

Two months after finishing my government year I finally had all the paperwork in order, and the village decided to have a grand opening of the health centre. First they held a Bingo event to raise some funds. Next they wrote letters to about thirty individuals asking them to be sponsors of the event. These invitees were special guests on the day, and were expected to put an envelope with a donation towards the work of the health centre in a box in return. They organised food and drink for the event, and bought a long length of white satin ribbon. On the day they sat the special guests on chairs in a big circle, and all of them held on to the white ribbon. The other villagers looked on from behind.

Speeches were made by the President of the village water project, one of the guests invited to sponsor the event, and myself. We spoke of the hard work and community spirit of all the villagers, the great contribution made by the team from the UK, and the wonderful opportunity it was for everyone to have access to health care on their doorstep.

Rachel, a team member who had stayed on to help in the village, was asked to cut the ribbon, and was presented with an engraved plaque expressing the thanks of the villagers to the team for their contribution.

The special guests were served a slice of pizza, bought as a special luxury from a pizza restaurant in town. Everyone else received a bread roll and cup of fizzy drink. Then sports were played; football both for men and for women, and volleyball. The whole community was there cheering on the players, and making the afternoon an occasion to remember.

The proceeds from the event were used to buy some shelves for the health centre. We were donated a couple of desks and an examination couch, and thus we were ready to open five mornings a week.

Our first patients were our regulars. Felicita came in for a new supply of insulin. "Here are the blood sugar results from the last month," she said handing me a piece of paper on which her son had recorded her results perfectly.

"You are doing great," I encouraged her. "We will stay at the same dose at the moment. Here are your syringes and insulin and the tablets you need. Tell your son he is doing a great job and to keep up the good work."

"Please accept these eggs," she asked me shyly as she turned to leave, "May God repay you."

Alicia came with a urine sample from Jeovhanny. "He is really unwell Doctorita, and this usually happens when he has a urine infection. Can you test it?"

"Yes of course," I replied, getting out the reagent sticks. "You are right he does have an infection here. I will go and get the antibiotic he needs."

"Thank you so much. Please accept this milk fresh from my cow in payment. You do like milk don't you?" She asked anxiously.

"Yes I certainly do, thank you very much," I assured her.

"I must dash or the milk truck will go back up the hill without me and I will have to walk," she explained, as she hurried out of the door.

Aida came with her cousin for her epileptic medicines. "Ah, Aida, I have been hunting out some new designs for your sewing. I think my Mum needs something fresh to sell now. Do you think you could make these spectacle cases? They would make great gifts for all those older people who need reading glasses." I explained as I pulled out a design I had done for them.

"They look really pretty," the girls gasped. "Yes we should be able to make some of them. How about we make a sample one and bring it to you to check?"

"That would be perfect," I smiled, "I look forward to seeing it."

I was happy at work, and rejoiced to count so many villagers as my friends now. I could see God at work in their lives and counted it a privilege to be able to live and work amongst them, to be able to show them God's love for them in practical ways. I felt fulfilled being able to use the gifts and talents God had given me for the good of others. But the nagging loneliness was also always present.

Vladimir had not taken my rejection at face value and continued to send me friendly text messages, asking how I was and telling me something of how he was getting on at work. He seemed so genuine; genuinely concerned for me, genuinely wanting to get to know me better and to be my friend. There was no trace of deception only support for me and the work I was doing.

He invited me to go and visit him for a weekend. I deliberated over whether to go or not for a long time. I prayed and felt only peace. I decided to go and see what happened.

Vladimir held his breath as he waited for my bus to arrive, not daring to believe I was really on it. As I stepped off the bus he took my backpack and walked with me to the river's edge, where we chatted and watched the boats go by. We sat down on some steps and he turned to speak his heart, still not daring to touch me. "Andy I would like to ask you to be my girl," he began nervously, "I know there are many differences between us, but I love you and would love to have the chance to make you happy."

I decided to be honest with him. "I came here to serve God and do His will. I feel so blessed by Him I want to share that love with the people in need here in Ecuador. I am not sure I will be able to do that if I am with you."

"But maybe God wants me to protect you and take care of you while you serve the people here. The people in the village are very fortunate to have you here to look after them. I support you in your faith and work."

As the peace of God enveloped my heart I had no hesitation in accepting his request, and we walked off along the river bank again now hand in hand.

Weekends became a welcome break from the work in the village when Vladimir would whisk me off to some new place of interest, to show me iguanas, take me to the beach or insist I try cow's hoof soup. We spent all the time we could together, and I enjoyed every second. His presence chased away any doom and gloom, and his touch made me feel loved and cared for. He became my best friend. "You are doing a great job," he encouraged me; "It is beautiful to see you so happy."

"I love being able to make a difference to people."
I answered. "Though there are things here that surprise
me and even scare me at times still."

One weekend Vladimir commented, "You seem very
sleepy this weekend. Have you had a hard week?"

"I know, I don't seem to be able to keep my eyes open,"
I agreed. "Maybe it is all the excitement of the new
health centre."

"And how are you getting on?" he enquired, anxious to
know if there were any problems.

"Oh, really well!" I replied. "I feel so excited each
morning to get up and go to work, ready to help those
who come along. It is really satisfying. Even the simple
things, like being able to give cute little Victor from the
orphanage some cream for an itchy rash he came with
yesterday. It all makes me feel so useful. I especially enjoy
treating those who come frequently. Even the seemingly
hopeless cases like poor old Don Sofonias. We have the
chance to get to know them well. It is wonderful to be
able to offer them hope, to be able to show them the love
of God a practical way."

"Your eyes light up when you speak about your
patients." Vladimir replied. "It is wonderful you can
use your profession in this way, that God has given you
this gift."

## CHAPTER FOURTEEN

# The Thin Blue Line

I sat, alone, staring at the thin blue lines on the positive pregnancy tests in shock. I had done two tests as I did not quite believe the first. How could I have been so stupid as to get myself into this situation? I asked myself. What was I going to do now? What were my family and supporters going to say when they found out? Should I go back home? But what should I do about Vladimir? Should I not give my baby the chance to know their father?

I sat caressing my abdomen, just wanting to hide away and enjoy every precious, miraculous moment of my baby growing and developing inside me.

But I knew I would have to face the music.

"Vlady, I have some news." I began. "I am expecting a baby."

"Ha, ha," he laughed, "You are not going take me in that easily."

"No, really I am serious. I really am pregnant. You are going to be a father."

"Really? You are not joking? You can't be serious?"

"Yes. It is true. I would not joke about this. I am going to have a baby." Tears welled in my eyes.

"I am going to be a father." Vladimir stated in shock. "I am going to be a father." He repeated in awe. "Hey Andy," he turned to look at me properly, "I love you and we are going to be the best parents ever." He assured me as the reality began to sink in.

It was not yet even general knowledge that we were dating, so the news came as a shock to our families too.

"You're joking right? You're not? Wow, you are going to be a Mum!"

"No, this is excellent; I am going to be an auntie. This is great news!"

"Well, whatever you decide to do we will do all we can to help you."

"Make sure you at least come here for the birth, you've got to look after yourself," my family responded as I told them one by one over the 'phone.

"Wow," I reflected as I took a deep breath, "I thought they would be upset with me. At least I can count on their support. That is a good start."

Vladimir's Dad took him off for a man to man chat with tears in his eyes, and then returned to give me a formal welcome to the family and offer me their unconditional support. "Who would have thought, this is your destiny," his Mum smiled kindly, immediately giving me a plate of soup to eat. "We will have to make sure this baby gets fed properly," she stated firmly. I could see a lot of soup eating ahead of me.

"You should go back to the UK immediately," colleagues warned me. "We have seen this happen before. Vladimir and his family only want the prestige and wealth of him marrying a white woman. It will all end in disaster. One colleague who married an Ecuadorian put up with him having affairs all their married life. Another married an Ecuadorian who turned out to be a drug dealer. Ecuadorian men cannot be trusted, they are expert in deception. You need to get out of here and reflect on things before making any decisions."

"Think very carefully before deciding to get married," the email from a supporter in the UK read, "cross-cultural marriages are very difficult. You would be better off raising the child alone."

"Sorry I can no longer support your work." Read several others.

"It was what I was expecting really, this kind of reaction." I told myself forlornly. "People have every right not to give me their support anymore if they think that this sin has ruined my witness as a Christian missionary. Maybe they are right. And I know that those who are warning me against Vladimir are just concerned for me. But it hurts all the same. The thing is none of these people know him, so how can they make these judgements about him?

I do feel I have let people down. People looked up to me, trusted me to live as a Christian Missionary should, and now I have failed them all. I have failed my Father in Heaven."

"Everyone is telling me not to get married," I told Vladimir bluntly. "They say Latin men are unfaithful and deceitful and you only want my money. They say we won't be able to make it work because we are from different cultures."

"To tell you the truth many of my family and friends are also telling me not to get married. To some extent it is true. You are from the north, from the other side of the planet; you eat different food and think differently to me. Our professions have nothing in common. But not all Latin men are the same Andy." Vladimir held me close, not knowing what to say to make sure I did not run off home, denying him the chance to know and hold the child he desperately wanted to have the opportunity to care for.

"I am so happy for you," read the email from a friend, "You have done so much for others you deserve to find happiness yourself."

"Well, at least there is someone who does not think I have gone beyond the pale," I thought, "it is lovely of them to write that. But I have been taught life is all about doing the right thing. It is not about seeking personal happiness."

Despite the cacophony of voices trying to advise me, I never doubted in my heart what course of action I wished to take. I loved Vladimir, and I loved our baby. I also loved this adopted country of mine, and the opportunities I had to serve its people. My desire was to stay right where I was and form a family with this gentle, patient man whose child I was bearing. I wanted to give my baby that most precious experience of growing up cared for by both parents. It was true that there were many differences between Vladimir and myself, but I could see no good reason why we could not make our relationship last if we both wanted to. I believed my baby had the right to know and be loved by their father. I was willing to take the risk of discovering I was mistaken in my estimation of Vladimir. I did not want to cause him or my baby the devastation of separating them with thousands of miles. I did not believe that was what God would want me to do either.

Mary gave me a long hug, and simply listened to my thoughts, hopes and fears, before answering the question that tortured me most. "Andy, you must not think that God can no longer use you here," she assured me. "Our God is a God of grace, who is in the business of forgiving sins, restoring brokenness and using us despite our failings."

I hoped she was right.

Vladimir invited me to go for a weekend with him to the beach. When we were bobbing up and down in the rolling waves of the warm sea, he turned to me and stated, "Andy, there is a reason why I cannot marry you."

My heart missed a beat, and I wondered wildly if he was already secretly married to someone else. I turned to him in confusion, while he continued, laughing mischievously, "It's because I haven't asked you yet!" Then he produced a sparkly ring and slipped it on my finger as he proposed, and I happily accepted. We lingered on the beach through the golden sunset, not wanting that special day to end, before reluctantly gathering our belongings and returning, hand in hand to the car full of fragile hopes and dreams for our future together.

I was made part of the family without hesitation. Vladimir's Mum fed me nourishing soups every day, concerned for her grandchild's development. I learnt to eat with a spoon and my fingers, though never quite mastered the art of leaving only a glistening white bone on the plate like the Ecuadorians.

Vladimir taught me how to cook rice Ecuadorian style; first washing the rice, then putting it in the pan and adding water, margarine and salt or a stock cube, bringing it to the boil, then lowering the heat to slowly allow all the water to evaporate, leaving fluffy white rice ready to be served. He then taught me to cook the staple dish, "estofado". This involved very finely chopping red onion, green pepper and tomato, stir frying them in a little oil, with either pieces of chicken on the bone, fish or beef. Once brown in colour stock, achiote, salt and coriander were added, and the ingredients simmered until the meat was cooked. It was served with rice. The art of a good "estofado" was in the chopping of the vegetables. They had to be minced to give a good flavour to the sauce. Ecuadoreans were practiced choppers, wielding their huge kitchen knives with expert precision. I nearly chopped my fingers off every time I had a go and had to resort to buying an electric mincer.

Vladimir tried lasagne, quiche, pizza, Yorkshire puddings, spaghetti bolognaise and shepherd's pie. He enjoyed trying new foods and flavours; it made life more interesting.

In Ecuador killing chickens and plucking them was women's work, as was gutting and scaling fish. Vladimir had to accept that I was never going to wring the neck of a chicken, though I did try my hand at gutting fish and shelling prawns. Likewise killing guinea pigs with a bop on the head and preparing them for cooking was done by his mother, and his sister killed one of her pet rabbits for the pot from time to time; beautiful white fluffy creatures, far too cute to end up in our stomachs. Once these animals were prepared I was happy to roast them, but I refused to do the slaughtering part.

As we spent time together with his family, I grew to appreciate their unity and spirit of cooperation. They were the souls of hospitality and kindness.

One sunny Sunday afternoon we went to visit Vladimir's Uncles and Aunts and cousins in a family gathering at his Granny's house. Everyone was enjoying playing football and eating soup and barbequed bananas together. One of his cousins, Alba, had a little baby boy. He started with "pujos", the Ecuadorian disease where a baby starts pushing out its tummy as if constipated. She told me that as her baby was a boy, I must be having a girl if

I had had that effect on him. While inwardly groaning at this prophesy, I reflected it was not long until I could have a scan to find out. In Ecuador you could walk into a radiology shop and request a scan at will. They were not even expensive. I was looking forward to finding out the sex of the baby soon.

I continued to work in the health centre, determined to continue to offer my service to God, despite those who thought I was no longer fit to do so. "After all," I reasoned, "the truth is I have never been fit to serve God. I have always been a sinner saved by His grace. That is the whole point of the gospel. I sin daily and am forgiven daily as I come before the cross of Jesus. I think my pride and selfishness are just as important in His eyes as what the world sees as "bigger" sins." I continued to pray that God might use me to show His love, that never changed or waivered, to those around me.

I continued to see people in tragic situations, whom I could in some measure offer comfort and help. Don Sofonias often popped into the health centre still, to request some painkillers for his now stiff and contracted arm, or to have his nails cut. We always tried to give him some time and attention, clean him up a bit and give him something to eat and drink. He sometimes sat in the waiting room to chat to others who were waiting, making the most of their company.

One day an elderly lady came in, filling the waiting room with an ominous smell. We took her through to the consulting room hastily, and found her leg to be the problem. Her daughter in law had brought her along, but said she preferred to stay outside – very unusual for Ecuadorians who usually accompanied their relative to see the doctor. As we peeled away her stocking and the dirty, smelly bandage underneath we were horrified to see a writhing mass of maggots covering and tunnelling into her entire lower leg. I had never seen anything like it. Monserrat, who was assisting me, did a stoic job of taking off all the soggy, repellent bandages, and then we took a step back to decide what to do next. The maggots were buried deep into her leg, and it was going to be impossible to simply pull them each off, so we plastered the whole thing in Vaseline in the hopes of suffocating them and bringing them to the surface.

I was thankful not to be suffering from morning sickness, as even feeling well it was hard to stomach.

"How did your leg get into this state?" we questioned her.

"I live alone and cannot see very well. My leg has been feeling uncomfortable, but I could not see what was wrong with it." The old lady told us. "My daughter in law came to visit and said there was a bad smell. She insisted on taking me to the doctor."

When we peeled off the gauze and Vaseline maggots fell like grains of rice onto the floor in their hundreds. I found a few escapees in corners for days to come. Despite our best efforts there were still hundreds more buried in multiple holes in her leg, so we applied a veterinary remedy to kill them, and asked her to return the next day. Neither Monserrat nor I felt much like lunch that day, and certainly did not want to eat rice.

The next day she returned with the remaining maggots now all dead. We patiently pulled them out of the caverns in her leg one by one with tweezers. They were plump and shiny white. They had obviously been doing well feeding off her flesh. We pulled away hundreds of the little beasts, and then dressed her wounds carefully, filling each hole and crevice with honey.

"It is such a relief my leg does not squirm anymore." The lady said, in what must have been the understatement of the year. "I slept well last night for the first time in ages."

Her leg subsequently healed up surprisingly quickly, perhaps because the maggots had left it so clean, without a trace of dead flesh. I was glad I was still in Ecuador, ready and able to help this poor old lady whom Jesus loved.

For days afterwards I could see writhing maggots every time I shut my eyes, and rice failed to be appetising for quite a while. Vladimir did not even want to hear about it; he was rather squeamish about such things. "No, no Andy," he protested, as I teased him with the gory details, "Don't tell me anymore. Let's talk about a nice generator I was battling with at work today."

A great granny in the village, Señora Maria, who was over ninety years old, developed skin cancer on her forehead. Her family took her to the cancer hospital for it to be operated on, but they were unable to remove it all, and the wound never healed. The family decided the old lady was too frail to withstand more treatment, and asked the health promoters to help them by dressing the wound. One of the ladies went to visit every day to wash and dress the ever growing wound on her forehead. The family did not want to see it: they did not have strong stomachs. I felt glad the ladies could use the training I had given them to now help their neighbour in this way.

The old lady was still walking around the house and patio when the health promoters started visiting. Gradually she walked less and less, and lost weight little by little, until she was confined to bed. The family did a great job of caring for her, feeding her soups and keeping her clean. We gave them pain killers to give her, and controlled the bleeding and smell from the cancerous ulcer. I felt it was a privilege to be in Ecuador still; to be able to be God's hands for that family. They had no hesitation in allowing me to love and care for them and to pray with them.

We heard of another lady suffering from cancer who lived far into the countryside. Monserrat and I set out one afternoon to visit her. We travelled to the end of the unmade road in the car and then, asking the neighbours for directions, set off walking across the fields towards her house. She lived on top of a hill, surrounded by cattle fields. I picked up quite a few "coloradillas" - tiny red bugs that attached themselves to my skin and itched like crazy.

When we arrived at the house Christina was surprised and pleased to see us. She was resting on the sofa in the sparse living room, reading her Bible. We introduced ourselves, and she shared with us the treatment she was going through. At forty five years old she was not ready to give up the fight against her cancer yet. She was undergoing chemotherapy, and commented, "The chemo costs so much I feel like I am trying to buy my life. We are selling fields to pay for it."

"How do you get to Quito for your treatments?" I asked her, concerned.

"My son-in-law takes me on a motorbike over the fields to the ranchera. I cross town to the bus terminal and catch a bus to Quito, then ride the tram to the hospital. After each treatment I have to do the same journey back home again often suffering from vomiting and pain."

"And how are you feeling now?" I asked, exhausted just thinking about such a journey.

"Mostly I worry about my daughters. I want to live to see them married and to enjoy my grandchildren. This is my youngest daughter. She is seventeen and looks after me and the house."

Her daughter spoke up, "Of course you are going to get better Mum. We will have lots of time with you yet."

I hoped she was right. I prayed with them before taking my leave and after that visit we did not hear from Christina for a while.

Señora Maria's condition worsened. The tumour on her forehead grew, invading backwards into her skull and brain. The family called me to go urgently to see her as she had gone unconscious. It was to be her final couple of days in this world, as she slipped quietly and peacefully away.

The family so appreciated having the support they needed from our team. It was very hard for families who had all the responsibility of caring for their relatives when they were diagnosed with a terminal illness. They were left to muddle on the best they could with no professional help. They had to become nurses overnight and learn how to dress wounds, give injections and enemas and to manage urinary catheters. Finding someone with know how willing to help them through this painful time was a literal Godsend. The health promoters did a great job of giving practical help, and also calm reassurance to this family. It was quite horrifying for them to watch as the cancer little by little ate away at their Granny's face. The health promoters kept the wound covered and enabled the old lady to retain her dignity and the affection of her family. I felt proud of them and the good job they had done. I felt that no matter what happened in the coming months the work I had started would continue in some measure.

One of Christina's daughters came looking for us in the health centre, asking us to visit her mother again. Her mother had now finished her chemotherapy and was dying. They had fought the disease against all odds and lost the battle. They could no longer deny the harsh reality. The girls wanted us to help them make their mother comfortable, and alleviate her pain.

Vladimir drove us up the long unmade road to visit her; concerned I should not be travelling such roads in my condition. When we arrived I saw immediately that she was in agony, and was glad I had made the effort to go. I never understood why the oncologists would tell someone there was nothing more they could do and send them home to die without any pain relief. Maybe they just never saw the patients suffer once discharged from their care, and did not realise what a difference some simple pain killers could make.

I gave her some morphine that I had with me, left over from a previous patient, and sent the daughters to buy some morphine patches that were now available in Santo Domingo. A fortnight's pain relief cost eighty dollars, the equivalent of eight days wages.

Her pain relieved, she slept for hours, catching up on the previous nights when her pain had not allowed her to rest. When she awoke she was much calmer and more relaxed. We visited again, and slowly, struggling now to find the energy to speak, she told us she just wanted to spend the time she had left in the company of her daughters.

They did an excellent job of caring for her and accompanying her day and night, making sure that she had all she needed, the older girls promising to care for their youngest sister. They gave all they had in caring for their Mum, knowing that the time they had left together was short.

And then the day came that they arrived on my doorstep to ask me to write the death certificate. Their entire community turned out to accompany the family through the night at the wake. The girls were not short of help to make the burial arrangements. Their friends and neighbours then helped them move forward again into the future.

"You know," I commented to Vladimir, as we sat listening to music later that evening, "you just never know what is going to happen next in life. She was so young to die; too young. The cancer robbed her of her chance to live to old age. We who enjoy good health should live every day to the full, and make the most of every opportunity we are given."

"The path through life is not how I thought, is not how I imagined," the music on the radio intoned, reflecting our sentiments that night. Our path so far had taken unexpected turns and we wondered what the next twist in the road would be. But we trusted God to accompany us along the way, to be our guide and our help.

## CHAPTER FIFTEEN

# For Better and For Worse

Mishel, one Aida's cousins, came to see me very excited one afternoon. "Doctorita, I have come top of my class, and I have been chosen to be the flag bearer in the flag ceremony this year. I would love you to come and watch me."

This ceremony took place on the same day in all the schools, and all those who were in their final school year had to take part and swear allegiance to the Ecuadorean flag. I looked forward to this new experience, to being part of this special occasion for Mishel.

The school lined up on parade in their best uniform; the girls with navy ribbons neatly tied around their necks, over their crisp white blouses, and the boys with navy ties done up smartly, matching their navy pressed trousers. They had highly polished black shoes on, the girls tottering in their high heels, and the flag party had white gloves on their hands. Mishel marched in bearing the flag, escorted by the second and third best students in her class. She made her way to the podium and read a speech out to all present with great confidence. Then she held the lowered flag while each of her class mates approached and kissed the flag, swearing their allegiance to their country.

Photos were taken of each child as they took part, and Mishel gave me one of her photos as a souvenir with great pride. She wanted to study to be a lawyer to defend the poor. Daughter of a man who had abandoned his five daughters, but persisted in stalking their mother, intimidating and threatening her, Mishel knew something of what it was to be on the receiving end of injustice. Mishel made her mother very proud that day. Her mother worked all the hours God gave to provide her girls with food, clothes and an education. Seeing the wide beam on her face that morning, I knew she considered it worth all that effort to see her daughter shine. I felt honoured they had thought to include me in their special day.

The sewing project had now expanded from being just Aida and her family, to include some ten other families with similar needs and problems. The women and girls gathered at my house to learn some new designs and blether.

This afternoon the conversation turned to their experiences giving birth. They recounted with relish the terrible pain they had suffered. "I was in labour for two days," Fredis complained, "It was agony and they just made me walk and walk in the hospital." The fervent agreement of the others present confirmed this was a common experience. No one had been given any pain relief of any kind. No gas and air, no morphine injections and no one knew what an epidural was.

Maria (Araceli's mother) stated that she had given birth nine times at home, and that two of the babies had died shortly after birth. Only her last baby had been born in the hospital. I was stunned at the matter-of-fact manner in which she recounted the deaths of her babies. It was not that she did not care, rather that she considered it was their destiny. It did not occur to her that had she had professional attention those precious children might have lived. Life and death was a matter of fate for her. She spoke with passion about the fight to raise her children the best she knew how, but was resigned to the fact that she had also lost babies to sickness. She considered this outside of her control, so there was no point in lamenting the fact. Twenty four children in every one thousand live births died before their first birthday in Ecuador, according to the World Health Organisation, compared to only five in Britain.

Sonja had had four children, and during the last caesarean section had been sterilised. "When my youngest child was a year old I started to feel unwell" she recounted. "My periods stopped and I was putting on weight. I went back to the doctor in the hospital who had done my sterilisation to find out what was wrong. He did a pregnancy test and an ultrasound scan, but said they were negative, just to go back and see him again in a month's time. But I did not know what was wrong with me so I decided to go and have another scan done by someone else. I was five months pregnant. I was devastated because I was planning to go and work in Spain with my sister for a while to send money back to my husband and children here in Ecuador."

"So what did you do?" I asked.

"I had to abandon these plans and wait for the baby to be born. He was born in the hospital but he was born with weak lungs, and died in the incubator a few hours after birth. It was better really that he was taken, as a sick child is too much of a burden."

I wondered to myself what had been the trouble with the little baby's lungs. Had he just needed some resuscitation? Had he lacked surfactant to make his lungs expand and work normally? What would have happened to that little boy had he been born in the UK? Maybe he would never have been the sickly child Sonja feared, just needed help to get started in life.

Sonja continued her tales of the hospital and recounted how her sister-in-law had had twin girls. "She went into labour, and was taken to the hospital and had birth pains for twenty four hours before a doctor took some notice of her. When he had realised she was having twins suddenly everyone sprung into action. Still not able to give birth naturally they carried out an emergency caesarean, but it was too late to save one of the babies. The larger girl survived, and the smaller was stillborn."

"Maybe it was for the best in the end," Fredis suggested. "It would have been very difficult for a single mother to look after twins and to work to provide for them."

"God knows what he is doing," Sonja agreed.

I rebelled against such fatalism. Having worked in a Scottish maternity hospital I had seen a woman's life saved by being transfused forty pints of blood, babies saved by timely caesarean sections, emergencies prevented by good antenatal care, and twins born at twenty four week gestation surviving in the neonatal unit. Maternity care in Santo Domingo was a different world entirely.

The health promoters were keen to share their experiences with me as well. Over cups of tea, when the patients had been attended to they filled me in on giving birth Santo Domingo style. Nora complained about the pain, the waves of relentless contractions, continuing for hours and hours, with no relief, just instructions to walk and walk until the baby came. At least she had had a safe delivery of her beautiful little girl, but she was too scared of the pain to try for another child. Monserrat said she had been too afraid of the hospital to go. She had had a relatively short labour with her son, and had stayed at home with her mother, refusing to leave the house. Hortencia had not managed to breast feed her babies, so had fed them watered down cow's milk: formula milks being too expensive.

Patients also loved to give me their pearls of wisdom. Felicita's husband told me to rub pig fat over my legs when I went into labour to give me strength. I thanked him for his advice, but privately thought it was more likely to make me vomit than empower me. Hortencia's mother, who had been a birth attendant in her time, advised me about cutting the umbilical cord. She claimed that if the baby was a boy you should cut the cord four finger breadths long, so that his penis would not be too small. If it was a girl you should cut the cord three fingers breaths long so that she would not be rebellious. I loved hearing these old wives tales. They made me giggle.

Their tales of child birth in Santo Domingo did scare me though. "It is no good," I told Vladimir in no uncertain terms, "There is no way I am going to give birth here. I am going home."

"But babies are born here every day," he protested, thinking I was exaggerating.

"And babies die here every day." I contested. "I want to make sure our baby receives the best care possible. I could not live with the regret should something go wrong here. I am going home."

"Well, we had better get on with the wedding first." He replied.

Planning a wedding in Ecuador did not take much time. The most time consuming was taking care of the legalities and paperwork required. I made my own dress from some embroidered gold fabric I found in the market street in town. Vladimir asked two of his cousins to be the witnesses, I handed in the paperwork to the registry office, and we were given a date and time to attend for the ceremony three days later. Vladimir's aunts, uncles and cousins travelled to be at the wedding with just a couple of days notice. There were no written invitations. Vladimir's parents decorated their house with white balloons, cooked up enough chicken and prawns for all the guests, and Mary made a huge chocolate cake. Everything was ready just like that.

I woke early the morning of the ceremony. Doubts fluttered in my mind. Was I doing the right thing? Everything had happened so fast. We had only been engaged for a month. We had not had time to get to know each other properly. There was still so much we were going to have to discover about each other. I recalled the conversation we had had when Vladimir had told me he couldn't ever see himself living in the UK. Was I ready to commit myself to living the rest of my life in Ecuador? Maybe we should have waited a bit longer before taking this step. But I could not imagine staying in Ecuador as a single Mum. If I was going to stay I needed Vladimir to be committed to me. Was Vladimir really the faithful, transparent man I believed him to be? Or would those who warned me it would end in tears turn out to be right? Only time would tell. I took a deep breath and patting my now rounded tummy said, "OK baby girl, here we go. I love and care for your Papi, and I think he is going to be an excellent father, so we are going to get married today, and I hope, I really hope, we are going to be a very happy family."

The brief civil ceremony was attended by close family only. Pushing down the twinge of regret that none of my family could be there, I appreciated Vladimir's Aunts, Uncles and cousins travelling through the night so that they could support him. We had a twenty minute slot, and had to arrive on time. We waited outside the door, while another marriage ceremony took place. As soon as the departing couple exited, we were ushered in. Those who arrived late, including Vladimir's Dad and Granny, missed it.

The room was quite dingy, grey and dull, with a giant cheesy love heart stuck to one wall. But the female registrar did her job with aplomb; standing to solemnly read the vows, then indicating all the places we and the witnesses had to sign. Vladimir's sister took some photos of the ceremony capturing some magic moments. After our first kiss as man and wife everyone crowded round to give us bear hugs and wish us well.

Having tied the knot we went to the shopping centre for ice creams while the lunch was being cooked. More cousins, Aunts and Uncles joined us there. Everyone was abuzz with the important occasion.

Meanwhile, back at Vladimir's house even more Aunts, Uncles, and cousins gathered to wish us well. Vladimir's builder friend Darwin and a few other special friends joined in. We entered the house hand in hand through the balloon archway, to great applause. Vladimir's father and mother both gave heart felt speeches and we were toasted in great style. Everyone came and spoke to us one by one, giving us hugs and kisses of congratulations.

Then people sat where they could find a perch to enjoy the food and the company. Mary's chocolate cake went down a treat, and she kept a motherly eye on the swelling in my feet after a day spent standing. It was obvious people were happy for us and wished us well.

We slipped away home early that evening, glad to be alone together at last and spent our honeymoon on the chicken farm where Vladimir worked. He had not been in the job long enough to be entitled to any holiday yet.

Vladimir hung up the hammock he had bought for me to rest in while he worked, and we talked about what our little baby girl might look like, and what colour eyes she might have. I could not believe my dream had come true. I had a little family of my own. I believed it was a gift from God, and it made me feel His love for me in a new and precious way.

## CHAPTER SIXTEEN

# Family Secrets

In a society where people did not have health insurance, car insurance, house insurance, nor savings for a rainy day, where there was no RAC waiting to come to the rescue, where the firemen often did not respond to emergency calls, and ambulances were scarce and had to be paid for, people had to rely on their families and neighbours for help when trials and tribulations came along. Those who lived in strife and conflict with others lurched from one disaster to another. Others who made the effort to live in peace with their neighbours and to help others, likewise found people rallied round them in their times of difficulty.

I began to discover I had not only married Vladimir, but had also become an integral part of his family.

I had already had to learn to be less independent, to give up my desire to be self-reliant, and to accept that I could not do everything myself. I now received less support from the UK and had to rely on Vladimir to help provide for me. I needed help to change the gas bottle on the cooker when it ran out, help from passers-by to know which road to take when out driving as there were no signs, and someone to accompany me when navigating the minefield of trying to obtain official documents.

Now not only would Vladimir help me with many of these tasks, but a member of his family would turn up to help me if he was unavailable. "It is such a relief to have people I know I can count on," I commented to Vladimir, "I know I am not alone. But it makes me feel that our privacy is invaded at times."

"What do you mean?" He asked, "They are family!"

"Well, they are your family. You are completely familiar with them all, but some of them I still hardly know. I do not really like them knowing all our business."

"They are your family too now, Andy." Vladimir assured me. "They are just helping us."

I knew they were just concerned for us but their unasked for advice still made me bristle sometimes. "You should not be driving, the baby will end up squashed," his Aunt reprimanded me. "You must not suck ice pops," another Aunt was scandalised, "You are going to give the baby a cold." "Oh how ridiculous," I thought as I smiled politely.

"My Aunt is building her house. I am going to go a couple of weekends to do the wiring for her, so I won't be able to come home those weekends." Vladimir informed me. He was still working away during the week on the chicken farm.

"Of course you must go and help her," was all I said, but inside I felt sad I was not going to see him for a fortnight. It was good he could help his Aunt and save her having to pay for an electrician, of course it was, but I was pregnant, hormonal, emotional and recently married and felt dismayed I had so little time with my husband. A little guiltily I hoped this kind of thing was not going to happen too often.

At least I had plenty to keep me busy and fill the time in his absence. I headed out to do some palliative care visits.

The first lady, Laura, lived in a small house in a slum built on an abandoned rubbish dump on the outskirts of town. Her son guided us to her house, where she lived with her daughter. Laura was in her seventies and was suffering from terminal cancer. She was in pain, had swollen legs and felt breathless. I gave her medications to help control those symptoms, and explained them all carefully to her attentive daughter. The family were obviously very poor. They had been unable to access treatment for their Mother's illness. Now it was too late to save her. But they were determined to look after her the very best they could.

Monserrat and I sat and chatted to Laura and her daughter that afternoon, getting to know them a little, and listening to their fears about what might happen to Laura. We tried to reassure them that we would do all we could to help and accompany them during this difficult season in their lives. I was happy to see she had such a supportive family. I knew she would be OK.

The situation the other patient we visited that afternoon faced was very different. She was a mother aged fifty, also dying of terminal cancer. She had about six children, all of whom now had their own homes except her youngest daughter who was only fourteen years old. This teenager was trying to look after her Mother with very little help from her older adult siblings. She had stopped going to school so that her Mother was not left alone.

One of her brothers lived two houses down the road, but he never visited. He was reputed to be a drug dealer. One of her sisters did pop in most days, but said her own family responsibilities did not allow her to spend more time with her Mother.

The family wanted us to donate them all the medicines we recommended to control their Mother's pain, but happily bought all kinds of expensive "natural" remedies which were lined up on the dresser by her bed. It was a divided family, who did not help each other willingly, filled with feuds and resentments.

In this atmosphere the patient, Rocio, lay in bed in pain. Her pain was not only physical but emotional and relational. She was becoming weaker daily, nearing her end, and we sought ways to help her and her family before it was too late.

The psychologist from Orphaids accompanied me on the visit and spent time conversing with Rocio's children, urging them to make their peace with their Mother while there was still time. She spoke with Rocio too, helping her accept her prognosis and addressing her fears. She shared her faith with her, offering her hope and comfort.

As I took in the effects of a dysfunctional family unit I felt ashamed at my reluctance for Vladimir to help his Aunt with her house.

Monserrat and I visited Laura again a few days later. We found she had suffered compression of her spinal cord by tumour that had spread to her vertebrae. She was now paralysed from the waist down, unable to move her legs and incontinent. Even if the problem had been diagnosed in time, the family did not have the wherewithal to have taken her to Quito for emergency radiotherapy to attempt to stop the paralysis. All we could do was to try to help her cope with her current situation.

We lent her a special mattress from the Orphaids store to help prevent pressure sores developing now that she could not move herself. Monserrat helped Laura's daughter to bathe her, and showed her how to massage and exercise Laura's legs.

Laura was resigned to what was happening to her body. She never once complained. She told us she had a strong faith in God, and knew He was with her helping her to cope one day at a time. She certainly seemed to be at peace. She kept her Bible at her side and told us it was a constant source of comfort to her. She asked us to read passages to her while we visited. She was one of the bravest ladies I have ever met. She gave me strength and fortitude by her example.

Laura was concerned for those around her. "I worry that my daughter is spending too much time looking after me. She is not spending enough time with her husband and children." She confided.

"You have to let her care for you at this time." We told her. "You looked after her when she was a girl and now she wants to be able to help you in your time of need. Her family understand."

"My son works long hours at the nearby recycling unit. He picks over the rubbish tipped on the dump each day, collecting anything that is recyclable. With his small wage he buys the medicines I need. He is very good to me too."

"That is how it should be. You cared for him and brought him up, now he is glad to be able to do something for you in return. You let him help." We urged her.

The family was a pleasure to visit. The sparse home was filled with love and affection, and they looked out for each other wholeheartedly. When Laura died the family spoke of how much their Mum would be missed. They were prolific in their thanks for the help we had given them, and immediately returned the equipment we had lent them.

My last visit to Rocio was very different. I sat on the bed next to Rocio who was very drowsy, but still able to hear. "We have a huge debt to pay at the cancer hospital Doctora," complained her older daughter. "How soon can you write the death certificate so they reduce the monthly payment due?"

"Let's focus on making your mother comfortable just now, and worry about that when the time comes." I remonstrated; horrified the daughter seemed so oblivious to her mother's feelings. "That is what is important at the moment."

I did not know what had happened in that family to cause such rifts and strife, but I knew that these conflicts had made a bad situation worse. It struck me as one of the loneliest deaths I had encountered. Rocio knew her children considered her an unwelcome burden to them, and I was sure that was what hurt her more than the physical pain she suffered. The whole scenario was tragic.

That evening, home alone, I was on the 'phone to Vladimir, "It is so essential to have the support of your family isn't it?" I commented. "Especially here, where there is so little professional help for these patients, if your family do not care for you, you have no one."

"Family is crucial." Vladimir agreed. "It is the most important thing, to help your family out in their time of need."

"I miss you," I sighed, "I wish you could be here with me, and feel our little girl kicking my stomach relentlessly. I think she is going to be a footballer."

"I will be there soon, a couple more days. You are fine."

The next day a different family scenario faced me in the health centre. An elderly man was brought in with his wife and daughter. His daughter asked me to examine him and to give him something for his abdominal pain. Their story of how long he had been unwell, and what previous treatment he had received was very vague. I was concerned that there was something seriously wrong with him, and asked them to take the old man for some tests. Once the older couple left the room the daughter stayed behind and told me the real story.

She had already taken her Father for tests and he had been diagnosed with pancreatic cancer. She had been told it was advanced, and no treatment was possible. She urgently whispered, "Now Doctorita I do not want my parents to know what is wrong. They would not cope; the news would finish them both off. I just need some strong pain killers to keep him more comfortable."

"I understand your fears," I told her, "but not letting your father know what is wrong with him has many implications. You are denying him the opportunity to put his affairs in order; maybe he has important things to say to some of the family before he becomes too weak to do so. In my experience it is extremely rare for patients to react as you fear; turning their face to the wall and dying all the quicker. Most patients, in reality, already know there is something seriously wrong. When a family talks openly about the diagnosis, they can console each other, hear the special words their loved one wishes to say to them, and care for each other better."

"But you don't know my parents, Doctora." She disagreed. "They are too old and frail to be able to cope with this bad news. It is better they do not know."

"Look, I will give your father something strong for the pain, but I cannot promise not to tell him his diagnosis should he ask me what is wrong with him. I won't force that knowledge on him, but should he, at some point ask me about his illness, I would respond honestly," I compromised.

She took the prescription but it soon became obvious she was never bringing her father back to see me.

"I hope they received the help they were seeking, and that the poor man did not suffer needlessly." I lamented a few days later to Vladimir, when he was finally home for a weekend. "I wish I could have done it better, won their confidence, and had the opportunity to help them more."

"Fear is a powerful thing Andy," he replied. "People here don't think like you do. That daughter was afraid she would not be able to cope with her parents' reaction to the truth. It is normal here for children to take the decisions for their elderly parents. It is seen as their responsibility to do so in fact. You have to tread very carefully. That daughter has to pay the medical bills for her father. Of course she has the most say in what happens to him. That is why the doctors told her the diagnosis, not her father. She has to decide what is best for her father according to her limited resources."

"But what about the right of her father to know what is happening to his own body? Shouldn't he at least have a say?"

"You might be right, but the role of the extended family is very important here. People rarely take decisions without at least consulting their families first. When they are old more often the younger generation simply make the decisions. You British people are very independent. That seems weird to us."

"I think life was simpler as a single girl!" I reflected. "All this living as part of the extended family takes some getting used to. I thought I was just marrying you and it turns out I have made a commitment to the whole lot of you!"

## CHAPTER SEVENTEEN

# Dilemmas

In Britain it is considered good medical practice for doctors not to treat their own family members. A doctor from outside the family is considered to be more objective, and doctors and their families are encouraged to register in a different practice to those they work in. In Ecuador expectations were completely the opposite. A doctor in the family was viewed as more trustworthy than an unknown doctor. They would have the best interests of the patient at heart, and would not be out to make money out of them. Using their knowledge and skills for family members was a way of helping them, saving them money and time, protecting them from doctors who might take advantage of them, and guiding them to the best solution to their problem.

I was happy to be able to help Vladimir's family in this way. There were so many things I did not want to help with – such as killing chickens ready for supper or cooking up a pot of stomach in peanut sauce for everyone to enjoy – that it was a relief to have some skill to offer them.

Vladimir developed an abscess in his leg. I took great satisfaction in lancing it and squeezing out the pus. He turned rather pale during the procedure, but had to agree it was a great relief when the pus was gone.

His sister fell off a motor bike. "Andy please can you clean my wounds up, my leg is a real mess. I don't want my Mum to see me like this or she will flip out. She is always telling me not to ride motorbikes." I cleaned up the dirt engrained wounds saving her a trip to the hospital - but the talking to from her Mum proved unavoidable.

"Why have you got a bit of plastic wrapped round your finger Dad?" Vladimir asked. "I cut myself on a machete today," was the nonchalant response. When the plastic was peeled away it revealed a gaping wound with the tendons exposed. I got my stitches out straight away. "I was hoping it would just stick together by itself," was the feeble protest of fear as the needle approached. He did have to admit being impressed at the neat result when I was finished.

"My Aunt needs an appointment at the cancer hospital in Quito. Can you help her? She will have to go at some unearthly hour of the morning to queue up to get one, and she has to travel hours to get to Quito in the first place," Vladimir appealed on her behalf.

I 'phoned a colleague who worked in the hospital and she managed to get the Aunt an appointment so that she would not have to queue up. It made the world of difference to the Aunt who was already tired and anxious.

A much more difficult ethical minefield was the expectation that I would issue doctor's certificates that I knew to be false. Often people had good reasons to be asking for them, and it pained me not to be able to help them beat the system in this way. They reasoned that the system was corrupt, so one had to use white lies to be able to achieve what was rightfully theirs. I suppose many doctors did sign such documents, to help family or for a fee.

"I don't understand why patients expect me to certify what we both know is untrue." I complained to Vladimir one evening. "Today a patient came along with a bundle of tests, all of which were normal. He asked me to write a doctor's certificate stating that he had a heart complaint. He said he needed it as evidence for a court proceeding. He was not pleased when I refused, showing him a normal electrocardiogram. I did not think writing a false certificate for use in the courts to be a good idea. What if it were challenged and found to be untrue? A doctor's signature only holds weight if it can be trusted to be honest. I cannot sign what I know to be untrue. I would be struck off in Britain for doing such a thing."

"Oh it happens here all the time. Nothing will happen to you here. I can understand why you don't want to do it, but people do expect it. They will think you are being unhelpful or problematic if you don't, especially if you refuse to do it for friends and family."

One of the health promoters asked me for a sick note for a friend's son who she said had had diarrhoea for a couple of days. He had not gone to work and his employer was now asking him to present a doctor's certificate. But I had never met the son, let alone seen him while ill. How could I write a certificate for him? She pleaded with me, saying, "Don't be a bad person Doctor, write the certificate for my son or he will lose his job and the family will not be able to eat." But I stuck to my guns. Why did he not go to a doctor the day he was sick if his employer required a certificate? Had he even been unwell or did he have some other reason for missing work that day? I felt awkward, even heartless refusing to do as she asked. She certainly piled on the pressure. But how could I write a certificate for someone I had never even met?

Vladimir came home, "Andy my cousin asked me if you can write him a certificate stating he was unwell one day last week when he missed work to go to a wedding. What should I say to him?"

The question hung in the air. This was family. These were the people who would help each other out, who would help me out, no matter what. Was his cousin going to be annoyed with Vladimir and me if I refused? More important to me, was Vladimir going to be upset if I refused? How could I make them understand I was not just being the awkward gringa with her weird ideas? "Maybe others would go ahead and do it." I thought. "There is virtually no risk of adverse consequences in Ecuador. The person receiving the certificate is very unlikely to query it, and anyway no doctors ever seem to lose their licence to practice medicine for much worse crimes. Goodness knows there are enough obstacles put in people's way daily barring them from making progress in life. Why not help them over a hurdle?"

But my British professional training and personal conscience simply did not allow me the luxury of helping out in this way. Being a trustworthy person, even if others did not always recognise me as such, was very important to me. "I am supposed to be a Christian missionary for goodness sake." I deliberated. "Whatever my failings at the very least I should be honest."

"I'm sorry my love," I began, "I really can't write the certificate. I would love to be able to help your cousin, but that just goes against my conscience, because it would be a falsehood." I looked at his face anxiously to see how he would respond.

"It's OK, you don't have to do it. I will think up some excuse to give him. Oh, that is him phoning me now. Let me have a chat with him."

I knew I was making things awkward for Vladimir and wondered if he really understood why I refused, or if deep down he just thought I was being awkward.

I was noticing he himself did not always tell me the truth, that I should not take literally all he said. His desire not to hurt feelings and save face won over being completely honest.

"I've cooked you some breakfast Vlady," I called one Saturday morning.

"Oh thank you, but I just have to pop out to help my Dad move some cement. I'll eat it later OK?"

When I caught up with him later it was to find he had eaten at his parents' house and had never intended returning for breakfast. "Why didn't you just say you didn't want breakfast?" I asked him, hurt he had not told me the truth.

"I didn't want to hurt your feelings after you had gone to that effort," he replied. I felt bewildered, not understanding his rationale.

And it did not just stop there. It was the same when talking to those who asked questions he did not want to answer. He made up an answer rather than admitting he did not have one.

Vladimir was on the 'phone to a friend, "Yes, I am doing well at work thanks, and yes Andy is expecting the baby soon. It is great to have a good job to be able to provide for the baby. At least I have a steady job, I don't want to lose it."

"But you are going to have to resign to be able to come to Scotland with me for the birth." I remonstrated; worried he had changed his mind. "And we agreed that you are going to look for work in Santo Domingo once we come back, so that you can live with me and the baby."

"Of course, Andy, nothing has changed, but I am not going to say all that to my colleague. I don't know how things are going to work out yet. I just tell him how things are at the moment. That is all that is certain."

"Why don't you just tell him you don't know, or to mind his own business if he is asking questions you don't want to answer?" I asked, perplexed.

"That just makes people ask more questions, or give advice you don't want to hear. It is best to just smooth things over with a little inventing."

"It is true that people do that here all the time. But it is so annoying! You can't trust anything anyone says. Like when a shop does not have what you are looking for and they say it will be there in a week's time. You go back in a week and they haven't even ordered it yet. They just say something, anything, to get rid of you. Don't do that to me too, Vlady. If you don't know, just tell me."

"Well, OK," he said, looking dubious, "But won't you then get upset?"

"No, I get upset when you tell me we are going to do something when you have no intention of actually doing it. I want to know what you are really thinking, not have my expectations built up only to find you never meant it."

Time was rushing on, and soon it was March. The Christmas post started to arrive, and I put the belated cards up on a string in the living room regardless. Along with them came some letters written several months before by concerned well-wishers offering all kinds of warnings and advice about the pregnancy and marriage. I put most of them in the bin. I was married now and it was too late to look back.

I was now seven months pregnant and starting to wear maternity clothes. I was thankful to have a neat bump, and to be keeping well. The heat did start to get to me though, in this hotter time of the year. I used to lie on the fresh tile floor, or under the fan on the ceiling to cool down. I spent lots of time in swimming pools and the river with Vladimir at the weekends, looking for anywhere that would cool me down. It was either that or taking to hanging out in the banks which were about the only places with the luxury of air conditioning in Santo Domingo.

I was still working, but was now having to take things easier. It was amazing to feel my baby girl moving and hiccupping inside me. Vladimir loved to feel her kicks, and to talk to her. When he was away working I would put the phone to my bump for her to hear his voice. We had chosen her names and now could not wait to meet her. It was all starting to feel more real, and very exciting. I started to count the days until my flight to Scotland. I was now anxious to be home, and for Vladimir to take a turn at experiencing my culture for a change.

## CHAPTER EIGHTEEN

# Antenatal Classes
# with a Difference

I was looking forward very much to seeing my family again after such a long separation. I wanted them to share in this extremely special occasion, the birth of their first grand-daughter and niece. I needed some molly-coddling from my Mum, and girly chats with my sisters. I felt like I was just about managing to withstand the pressure of constantly having to interpret my daily experiences through the filter of another culture. It was still an effort to live and work in a foreign language and fit in with alien customs. Once back in Scotland that stress would be removed, and I would be able to relax, knowing how to speak and behave without having to think about it anymore. All the tension of the recent months would just melt away.

I was looking forward to soaking in a hot bath, having to put on a woolly jumper, eating some melt-in-your-mouth milk chocolate, and watching the BBC on television. I could not wait to eat some Scottish sausages, baked beans and hot toasted cinnamon and raisin bagels with plenty of melted butter. It was going to be heaven.

I set about organising the projects I was leaving behind. The health promoters were organising themselves to continue to do what they could in the health centre. We had a class one afternoon a week in the weeks before I left going over the most important skills they needed. We talked about the treatment of children with coughs, colds and diarrhoea. We reviewed the treatment of those who were currently attending for dressings, so they could keep these treatments going. We went over the advice they should give to those using pills and injections for family planning. We practiced first aid for cuts, animal bites and burns. We spent an afternoon going through the tablets, creams and syrups they were competent to prescribe, using the formulary I had written for them.

"It has been really good to have these classes before you go Doctorita," Monserrat spoke for them all, "we feel much more confident about doing the job now while you are gone."

"It is good I am still going to be able to come for my insulin while you are away Doctorita," said Felicita on her monthly visit, "but I shall miss you not being here. I hope I do not become unwell."

"You look the picture of health at the moment," I encouraged her, "and your diabetes is well controlled now. Just make sure you keep looking after yourself and taking the medicine."

"Do come and visit Jeovhanny before you go Doctorita," Alicia implored. "It is a long time since you came to see us now. The plants are much bigger and the girls are both doing well at secondary school."

"I will do my best to come," I promised, wondering how I would fit it in.

"I do have a favour to ask you," continued Alicia uncertainly. "Jeovhanny has been using this same tracheostomy mask since he left hospital and I cannot find any to buy here. He needs a new one. Do you think you could find one while you are in the UK?"

I took the old, yellowed mask in my hands and turned it over, "Yes I am sure I can. Let me take a quick photo of it to make sure I get the right thing."

"We hope all goes well for you, that your baby is born safely, and that you do not delay in coming back to us," Nora chipped in.

"The patients are going to miss you. It will not be the same at all without you. Make sure you come back again quickly."

Giving them all hugs and kisses, I left them to go it alone. They continued to supply the regulars with their repeat medications for diabetes, high blood pressure and arthritis. They treated their neighbours for minor complaints and injuries. They helped the women maintain their family planning and continued to dress leg ulcers. They went to town to buy the new supplies of medicines. The income from the sales of medicines had to cover the cost of buying future stock. They worked in pairs, helping each other if they were not sure what best to do, and keeping each other company on quiet mornings. I was sure they would do a good job, and also importantly that they knew the limits of what they were capable of.

The sewing ladies and girls all came to my house several afternoons in a row to learn the designs I was giving them to make during my absence. They made samples of the Christmas stockings, table mats, bags and decorations they were to make, and I made sure they had sufficient materials of the right colours on hand as well. They each had their list of items to make and Mary graciously agreed to receive the goods when made and give them their payment.

I was so encouraged to see how much their sewing skills had improved over the past months, and more importantly their self-confidence too.

"I was so nervous at first," reminisced Maria, Araceli's mother. "It was so hard to do the designs well and I made so many mistakes. It seemed to take me forever to make the purses. Now I am so much better. I am really enjoying the sewing and am so glad to have this income. I don't have to send the children out begging for food anymore. I can now afford to buy it."

"And how are all the children getting on at school?" I asked.

"They all passed their school year except Araceli. She is going to have to repeat the year. It bothers her, her blind eye you know, and she just doesn't seem to take in what the teacher is explaining."

"Why don't we see if we can give her some extra help now in the holidays?" I suggested, "Maybe she needs someone to explain things to her again one to one."

"That would be wonderful, but who is going to have the time to do that with her?" Maria wondered.

"I have an idea," I stated, planning to speak to Vladimir's cousin who had finished secondary school. She had great patience with children and time on her hands. I was sure she would do a great job.

"We are going to miss you while you are away," commented Fredis shyly. "I have learnt so much through the sewing afternoons. I cannot believe I know how to use a sewing machine now. I would never have thought six months ago that I would be able to make these beautiful embroidered hand-bags. I am so glad to be part of this group."

"And we are so glad to be able to study secondary school," piped up Tania and Jenny, "Don't stay away long."

"I am going to take all these lovely things you have made with me to Scotland in my suitcase," I told them, "and when I see my friends and family I will tell them about you all and how purchasing one of your beautiful handmade items helps you feed, clothe and educate your children. I am sure they will want to help by buying something."

"I feel so much better now I can take my medicine regularly," Aida smiled. "I hope you will not stay away long so that I can keep on sewing."

"Of course I will come back," I reassured them, "Just think how far we have come. It all just started with Aida needing her medicine and now there are ten of you stitching for your families and your education. I am not abandoning you. I will be back," I promised.

I popped into Orphaids to visit the orphans and to say my good-byes. They all gathered round to pat my tummy and wish me well. "Can you just take a look at Victor, while you are here," they asked, "He hasn't been so well the last few days. Just a cold really, but he hasn't been able to shake it off, and he just seems to lack energy." I gave him a check over and asked when his next appointment at the HIV clinic was. "Next month, he will be due his blood tests then and they will review his medicines."

"Make sure you keep the appointment," I recommended, and gave little Victor a special hug. I would miss his smiley face and gentle ways.

Vladimir's Mum heard that Jacqueline, Araceli's older sister, was about to turn fifteen years old, her coming of age. No one in her family had the resources to throw her a party, so Vladimir's Mum decided to organise one. She took her to town and bought her a pink dress and shoes. Jacqueline looked like a princess, and if the wide smile on her face was anything to go by she felt like one too. Then Vladimir's Mum set about cooking a meal of fried chicken, salad and chips: enough for all of Jacqueline's family. She roped me into cooking a birthday cake, which I iced with pink icing and heart shaped sweets. I also took along a pink cushion with a radio inside for a present. Jacqueline, together with her Mother, brothers and sisters all enjoyed the feast, posed for the photos, and had an evening to remember. It was an evening filled with shy pleasure, jokes and laughter, smiles and tears. Jacqueline was so sweetly surprised and thrilled to have such a celebration of her special day, when she had not been expecting it to be different from any other day. I hoped it would be a memory she would cherish for many days to come, a jewel in her otherwise troubled childhood. It seemed a fitting note on which to make my departure.

"Well, Lord, this is it," I prayed as I left Santo Domingo. "I am leaving behind this work You have given me for a while. I hope what I have done here has pleased You and brought You glory, and I leave all these dear people in your hands."

I went to the chicken farm to spend a week with Vladimir before leaving for Scotland. He was booked to follow me a month later. It was a blissful week. I spent my time swinging in the hammock, rereading a favourite book, indulging in pure relaxation. Out there in the countryside it was so peaceful; the insects made the most noise. It was hard to get phone reception. There was no internet. We were free to simply spend time together with no other demands on us.

When I arrived at the farm in the car, Vladimir greeted me with great excitement. He had been out with the herdsmen and had managed to film a cow giving birth to her calf on his mobile phone. This was his version of an antenatal class, and he was itching to show me what I was about to go through. "Only a man would think this is a helpful thing to do," I shook my head in mock despair.

Having graciously watched his film of a calving we went out to the nearby village to eat. Vladimir had hosepipe soup (so called because of the stuffed cow's intestines it contained). I stuck to the soup with an identifiable chicken leg sticking out of it. I did not feel in the mood for adventurous eating. We then wandered along the river bank, holding hands and talking about all that was about to happen to us. These were such pleasant moments, our chance to dream about our future together, our tiny baby and what the days ahead would hold. I was very happy to be about to see my country and family again soon, and Vladimir was excited to have the opportunity to travel to Britain for the first time.

The week passed too quickly. Our uninterrupted time together came to its end, and we set off for Quito so I could catch my flight. Blowing Vladimir a last kiss as I went into the departure area, I turned my thoughts to Scotland. So much had happened since I had last been home. When I had set out for Ecuador three years before I had never dreamed I would be returning with a husband and baby in tow. It had all happened so fast sometimes I still thought I would wake up and find it was all a dream.

## CHAPTER NINETEEN

# A Bundle of Joy

Being back in Scotland was somewhat surreal at first, and I did wonder if I were in a dream. Some things did not appear to have changed since before I had left. My parents' house had its same familiar smell: it felt so normal to be there. I went back to using a debit card when shopping, looking for the postman to arrive each day, and eating roast dinners with surprising ease. It was incredible to have high speed wireless internet available twenty four hours a day, and to be able to phone up and chat to friends I had not talked to in a long time. It was refreshing to be able to simply drink water from the tap, and wander down the street without watching for pickpockets.

Other subtle changes sometimes caught me out; a new style of bank note, my winter clothes being out of fashion, and discovering the new television phenomenon "Britain's got Talent". I had forgotten how materialistic Britain was, how much stuff people had cluttering up their homes. I had forgotten how many unused things I had cluttering up my parents' home. Suddenly it seemed to me incongruous when folk complained about the care they received in the wonderful NHS, free of charge, or how the state was not taking responsibility for their Granny in her old age. Now I had spent so much time with people who expected to pay for the little health care they could afford, and who took on the responsibility to care for sick relatives at home with great bravery and compassion, I was simply grateful for all the professional care freely available in the UK. It was amazing.

It was wonderful to be embraced by my family in every sense of the word. My Mum was so excited to be about to become a Granny. She took me shopping in Inverness for baby things, and I indulged in the seemingly inexhaustible choice of clothes, shoes and toys on sale. It was almost paralysing seeing the sheer volume and variety of goods on sale. I could not help but compare it to the market street in Santo Domingo with its stalls full of poor quality but relatively expensive goods. The Primark phenomenon meant cheaper yet better quality clothes were on sale in Scotland than in Ecuador. Toys sold in Britain certainly had to be made to a much higher standard than they were in Ecuador.

My siblings had prepared a baby shower of presents. They presented me with nappies, wipes, talc, shampoo, baby grows and teddies. They had also persuaded friends to lend me a Moses basket and baby bath for the duration of my stay. They all came to see me soon after I arrived, excited to be able to catch up on three years' worth of news. I knew that they loved me very much, and thanked God for this family He had blessed me with.

Friends came to visit me as well. With so many it was just like no time at all had passed since we last saw each other. We picked up our friendship where we left off. These were the friends who stuck by me no matter what. Friends who supported me and the work I was doing out in Ecuador. Friends I would be forever indebted to.

However despite the closeness of our friendships there was so much I could not hope to explain. I could recount some stories of life abroad, but could never really put into words the experiences I had lived through, let alone the subtle ways it had changed my heart and thinking. I hesitated to express some of what I truly felt on returning to my home country. I did not want to appear to be criticising these good people who were simply living life the way they thought best in their own context. I could not expect them to have the same desire to help the poor old couple living under plastic held up by bamboo when they had never met them nor seen their appalling living conditions. They would not understand the repugnance I felt at the many items that were treated as disposable in the UK, when they would have been repaired and re-repaired in Santo Domingo until they were truly unusable. Bags with broken straps were sewn back together, shoes were repaired multiple times, and clothes were patched and refashioned. I had been brought up short myself when I noticed my neighbour wearing clothes I had thrown out in the rubbish hole in the garden. I discovered she often rummaged through the garbage heap in search of items she could make use of. In Britain it was often cheaper to buy a new one than to repair the old one.

I went to speak in some churches about the work in Ecuador. I tried to bring the people I had met there to life with photos and stories, and sold the crafts the ladies had made helping to raise funds to continue the project on my return. It was touching to see how people responded wanting to help these people they had never met. They asked insightful questions, and took a genuine interest. Often people donated more than I asked for the craft goods with great generosity. I was moved by people's willingness to support the projects in Ecuador, many giving sacrificially to help those less fortunate than themselves.

My tummy grew ever bigger. It seemed to suddenly expand in that last month. Maybe the abundance of cakes and pies available had something to do with it. Vladimir chatted to me over the internet most days, and was counting the days until he would be able to join me. We hoped the baby would not decide to come early, so that he could be there for the birth.

The day he arrived in Aberdeen airport I was waiting anxiously by the arrivals area. Everyone else off his flight came through, and still he did not make an appearance. I was having nightmares of him having got lost in the huge Amsterdam airport where he had had to change plane, when an air hostess off the flight came through, and seeing my anxious face asked me if I was waiting for a "small dark man?" I nodded and she continued saying not to worry he was just chatting to the immigration officials.

Eventually Vladimir was allowed to enter Scotland, and he arrived looking rather flustered, "I didn't understand a word they were saying to me, their accents are so different! This is going to be harder than I thought!" He exclaimed as he greeted me warmly.

It was interesting to see Scotland through his eyes. He thought the countryside was beautiful and loved being able to see seals, highland cows and deer. He decided fresh Scottish Salmon was perhaps the most delicious food he had ever tasted, and wanted to eat it every day. "I cannot get over how the cars stop to allow us to cross the road on a zebra crossing." He remarked astounded, "And all the traffic lights work all the time. The roads are all surfaced, well maintained and fast without any pot holes. No one steals the manhole covers. It is amazing!"

My brother and sister took us on a trip up the Cairngorm so he could experience snow, and to a distillery so he could see where the famous Scottish whiskey was produced. He thought it was incredible and took hundreds of photos.

He thought the Scots cold hearted because they did not greet each other with a kiss. "Andy, get up and give your Mum a kiss," he reprimanded me shocked when I did not get up to embrace my Mother when she arrived to pick us up from my sister's house. He thought my simple "Hi Mum" was incredibly rude.

"It is so tiring struggling to communicate in English all day long Andy. Was it like that for you when you were learning Spanish?" He asked me.

"Oh yes, it is exhausting," I agreed; "Now you are getting to experience what it is like for me to live in a different country."

He admired the amazing white sandy beaches near my sister's home, but could not get over how cold the sea was. His feet ached with the chilliness of paddling in the water. "I could never have a swim here," he complained, "Give me the warm Pacific Ocean any day!"

He did not appreciate being given cereal for breakfast or sandwiches for lunch. He felt hungry all the time. I found some microwavable packets of flavoured rice in the supermarket and these became his staple food.

The weather was kind to us that May, and we enjoyed many sunny days, warm for the time of year, and those light mid-summer evenings when it seems like the night is never going to arrive. Coming from the equator Vladimir had never known it still be light at ten o'clock in the evening. Back in Santo Domingo the sun set at half past six every single evening of the year.

Tamara was born three days after Vladimir arrived. It was a beautiful sunny day. Light streamed in the window as she made her start in the world. I was so appreciative of being in a clean, efficient well-equipped hospital, with well-trained experienced staff. The midwives were wonderful, and gave me every confidence in them. The birth took place without complications, and the gas and air did its job perfectly. I stayed in the hospital a couple of nights while the midwives helped me to establish breastfeeding. I was completely satisfied with my care and very thankful for all the staff did for me. I was so relieved not to have given birth in Santo Domingo. I shuddered at the thought.

As I held my own precious tiny bundle that first night, I felt a sense of awe. It seemed incredible to have been blessed with such a perfectly beautiful little daughter. I wanted to hold her tight and just enjoy the delicious feeling of having her secure in my arms. I gingerly dropped a kiss on her soft forehead, smelling her delightful baby smell and gazed at her until I fell asleep worn out.

I was completely unprepared for how exhausting looking after a new-born baby was. Tamara had a good set of lungs and liked to use them frequently. I was very grateful to be at my parents' house, and to receive their help in the days that followed. The local midwife also came to visit several times to advise me on breastfeeding and to do Tamara's heel prick test. None of these services were available to Ecuadorian women who were sent home without any follow up.

"I can see why Ecuadoreans have the forty days of rest after child birth," I commented to Vladimir, "it takes some getting used to, this new baby thing."

Vladimir was concerned when I suggested venturing out for a walk a few days after giving birth. In Ecuador new mothers did not leave the house for a month after child birth. They stayed in bed as much as possible, and a female relative attended to the household chores. One patient in the health centre in Ecuador had told me her mother-in-law had insisted she have "forty days under the mosquito net." Not even showers were allowed. She had longed for the day she could finally go and bathe in the river. I persuaded Vladimir I was quite able to walk, and we wandered along the road with the pram, enjoying the fresh air, purple mountains and gently grazing sheep.

The postman brought presents from well-wishers every day. I think all my friends and family, and all my Mum's friends too must have sent us a gift for Tamara. We ended up with enough clothes to kit her out for the whole of her first year, and to give away to various Ecuadorian cousins who had baby girls shortly after us. People were very generous. Feeling somewhat overwhelmed Vladimir reflected, "Some babies are born into a world of plenty: they will never lack for anything and will have more besides. Other babies will never know what a toy is, own a storybook or have anything other than second hand clothes. We are so privileged to be those who have received much in life; love, education, good examples and encouragement."

"Indeed we continue to receive so much help and support from many people." I agreed. "I hope we can be the kind of parents who give that same love, care and attention to our daughter, and teach her to do likewise."

There were many firsts to be celebrated. My Mum showed me how to give Tamara her first bath. She had her first cuddle with her Grandpa. There was the first time we took her for a walk in the pram, and the first time each of her five Aunts and Uncles came to visit. She had her first passport photo taken when she was barely a week old, and was registered in the local registry office with both her father and her mother's surnames, as is customary in Ecuador.

We wanted to show off something of Scotland to Vladimir during his stay, so started venturing out on trips. We spent an afternoon at the Eilean Donan castle, enjoying imagining how people had lived in times gone by. We went for a ride on a glass-bottomed boat, looking out for fish, seals and otters. My Dad took Vladimir for walks on the Isle of Skye, and my brother took us on a drive to Applecross, where we saw translucent jelly-fish floating in the sea, and ate the World's Best mouth-watering fresh fish and chips. We visited the Glenelg brochs: ancient dwellings, thousands of years old. A neighbour invited us round for Vladimir to have a go at playing the bagpipes, which turned out to be a hilarious experience. He was totally unprepared for the amount of puff he needed to be able to get a sound out of them – I say sound advisedly as the noise he managed to produce could not in all honesty be called music. The lad whose pipes they were then gave us a demonstration of how it was really done, much more tunefully.

We enjoyed the West Coast tradition of people putting money in the pram. As we walked around the shops in the village where my parents lived acquaintances would want to have a look at the baby and would then slip a fiver in the pram for us to buy something for her. "We should go out for a walk round the village every day," Vladimir joked.

We had to travel to London to register Tamara in the Ecuadorian Embassy. This was to ensure she received dual nationality and avoided any problems in immigration on our return to Ecuador. We travelled by train down to London. There were only a couple of tourist trains in

Ecuador, so these modern, high speed smooth running machines were something of a novelty for Vladimir. "I can't believe you travelled to school on these swish trains." He marvelled, "I had to bounce to school and back on the rickety ranchera."

The Ecuadorian Embassy was in Trafalgar square, so it gave us the chance to view some of the famous sights of London that were nearby; the Houses of Parliament, London Eye and Tower Bridge. Vladimir took plenty of photos so that he could show his family back home.

We marvelled at the cost of a cup of coffee. The same amount back in Ecuador would have paid for meals for a whole day for the both of us. Similarly the cost of public transport was wildly more than the subsidised buses of Ecuador, though admittedly also more efficient, clean, faster and more reliable. There were no rickety rancheras to be seen in London, filled to overflowing with sweaty people, chickens squawking, sacks of pig food and heads of bananas.

We made our way to Edinburgh, where I had studied medicine and still had many friends. I felt so at home back in my old haunts, gazing up at the ancient castle while taking a walk through Princes Street Gardens, the paths lined with brightly coloured flowers in bloom. Vladimir filmed a man playing the bagpipes, and bought a postcard of a man in a kilt as a souvenir.

My friends gathered together one afternoon, eager to share news and have a hold of Tamara. It was fun chatting together, meeting some of their children for the first time, and munching away on delicious home-made tray bakes that no one can make better than the Scots. Tamara received a fluffy sheep bearing the Scottish flag, and a toy puffin to remind her of her Scottish roots.

Back at my sister's house near Elgin we prepared for the wedding blessing we had organised for our final weekend in Scotland. My close family, Aunts and Uncles, Vladimir's brother Frank, who was still living in Spain, and my closest friends all made their way to Elgin for the special occasion. John and Brenda Hart, the missionaries who had inspired me to work in Ecuador in the first place, came to lead the ceremony. It was to be conducted in both English and Spanish.

The blessing took place on the beach that light, warm evening in June. The ceremony was personal and informal. The family gathered round us, as we repeated our vows, and also pronounced a blessing on baby Tamara. It was a public recognition of our new family unit, a chance for us all to be together and to celebrate.

We chose barbequed salmon for the meal that followed, eaten as we mingled and chatted together outside, the breeze brushing our cheeks as it blew up off the sea. We concluded the evening in a local hotel, cutting the ornate cake my Mother had made, and presenting humorous awards to the new Grandparents, Aunts and Uncles. It was good to be together and we made the most of the party.

Over the next couple of days family members took their leave as they had to head back to their respective homes, and the good-byes mounted up. We started packing our cases, squashing the abundance of gifts we had received into our allotted baggage allowance, preparing for the long journey back to Ecuador. I tried not to wonder how long it would be until we saw everyone again.

We were ready to go back to Santo Domingo. "You know my love," I began, "It has been a wonderful trip, most of all the chance to spend time with my family, but now I am ready to get back to "normal" life. Tamara is almost six weeks old and settling more into a routine. It is time for it to be just the three of us, in our own home: for us to start our family life together. This will be the first time we have been able to live together as a family."

"It is time for me to find a new job." Vladimir agreed. "I have loved visiting Britain and meeting your family, but it is hard work trying to talk English and get used to your strange ways. I want to go home, eat cow's stomach, listen to Latin music and swim in the river."

"What do you like about Britain?" I asked.

"I like the efficiency and organisation. It is so much easier to achieve things here. Scotland is very beautiful. But the people do not show much affection, they are too cold for my liking. Not even you give Tamara kisses."

I laughed, "Well I don't kiss her on the mouth like you do, it isn't hygienic: I might give her an infection."

Vladimir fell about laughing, "That is the most ridiculous thing I have ever heard." He chuckled, "Everyone back home kisses babies. You will find out soon!"

"Oh dear," I sighed, "You Latinos are so sentimental. You just do what your hearts tell you and don't use your heads."

Departure day arrived and the hardest thing was saying goodbye to my Mum. Tamara had two Grannies that loved her very much, and she was going to grow up knowing one very well, and the other only from a distance. There was no way of changing that, and I felt so sad that my Mum was no longer going to be able to give Tamara cuddles, tell her little stories or rock her to sleep.

The one comfort in the inevitable sadness of parting was the knowledge that my sister Rachel had already booked a flight to come and visit us. It was marvellous to have that visit to look forward to, to know that Auntie Rachel would be arriving to see her niece in the near future. I knew that the time would fly by.

We travelled back to Ecuador on the same flight as the sister of the then President of Ecuador. Seeing our tiny baby she chatted to us and asked to hold Tamara, so we playfully snapped a photo of them both. She took us to the front of the queue and commandingly made sure we were first onto the plane.

Settling down for take-off Vladimir and I held hands and looked at each other in excitement. This was it. We were going back to our home together. Holidays and travels were over. It was time to form our family together, and take care of this amazing, precious little girl who was asleep on my lap. We were full of optimism could not wait to get started.

## CHAPTER TWENTY

# Plump and Beautiful

Every day with our little baby was an adventure. Every day she changed and grew, and developed new abilities. There was the first time she gave me a smile, and later her first delightful chuckle. There was the way she started to take an interest in her surroundings, hold on to my finger, and rattle toys. She was my constant companion.

Looking after a baby was the hardest thing I had done in my life. Being a first time Mum to one little girl was more difficult to cope with than setting up a health centre. It was utterly draining. It was more tiring than working one hundred hour weeks as a junior doctor, because it was more relentless. I could never take a break. I had to get up in the night every night when she wanted a feed. Broken sleep for weeks on end was taking its toll. During the day I was constantly at her beck and call. She was tiny and helpless, and I had to work out why she was crying and try to resolve the problem for her. Sometimes I had done everything I could think of; changed her nappy, given her a feed, changed her clothes, rocked her in the pram, and still she cried. I did not know what else she wanted. She demanded my attention all the time.

I never had a moment to myself. When she finally fell asleep at night I did too.

The first few days I was home I received many visitors. One afternoon the sewing ladies came on mass to welcome me back and to admire the new arrival. "Please accept this chicken," Fredis asked me as she handed me a freshly plucked offering.

"Thank you that is so kind," I replied, knowing Vladimir would appreciate a homemade chicken soup with boiled green banana and herbs - a favourite of his.

"I am sorry I could not bring you a chicken," apologised Maria, Araceli standing shyly with her mother, "I only had these eggs to bring you."

"Thank you very much; it is so kind of you to bring them." I replied warmly, knowing that they needed them more than I did.

"You are looking so fat," they all agreed, approving smiles on their faces.

"They mean it as a compliment, they mean it as a compliment," I repeated to myself as I forced myself to smile. Being plump to them meant health and wealth and happiness. As soon as they had gone I started to hunt out the postnatal exercise DVD I had brought back with me.

The health promoters came another afternoon, complete with chickens, and cooked a meal to welcome us back. They just took over the kitchen, wielding their huge kitchen knives as they expertly sliced up portions of chicken to fry, and peeled, chipped and fried potatoes at a great rate. While they cooked they filled me in on how they had gotten on while I was away. "Felicita has come each month for her insulin; she seems to have kept well. She is planning to bring you a chicken to welcome you back. Alicia came to ask if you were back yet because she needs the new oxygen masks you promised to bring her. Don Sofonias has been popping in as usual. He had another stroke while you were away, but got back on his feet again quickly this time. He continues to limp up and down the road looking for people who will feed him."

"So how did you get on in Scotland? Tamara is such a precious little baby. We are all going to want plenty of cuddles. You are looking really well. You are much fatter than you were. Scotland must suit you." I gritted my teeth and managed to thank them for their compliments, inwardly resolving to start my post-natal exercise video as soon as possible, and to stop eating cakes.

I went back to work in the health centre a week after we arrived back. "This is why I am in Ecuador, after all, to work and help the people." I said to Vladimir as I prepared for my first day back. I thought I would go stir crazy if I stayed at home. I enjoyed my work. It was my purpose in life. I also felt duty bound to continue what I had started. I did not want to be a failure, to let people down. I wanted to continue to use the skills God had given me to serve Him.

I walked down the road with Tamara in the pram, and she accompanied me all morning while I attended patients. The health promoters helped entertain her by turns, and patients were itching to steal a cuddle. Her clear blue eyes were much admired. Everyone had an opinion on which of us she resembled. Most came out in favour of me due to her white skin and light brown hair, but some were equally definite she resembled her father or another member of the Ecuadorean side of the family.

Vladimir was right. Every Tom, Dick and Harry gave her kisses and cuddles. "She is going to get every cold going at this rate," I complained to Vladimir that evening.

"Don't be silly, she will develop resistance. Babies need kisses. I am more worried someone might go off with her. Don't ever let her out of your sight will you?"

A shiver went down my spine; that did not even bear thinking about.

All my patients offered me unasked for advice. It seemed Tamara was public property and everyone had the right to comment on her upbringing. "Doctorita, she is crying because she is hungry. Why don't you feed her?"

"But I just fed her. She has wind that is all. She will be alright in a moment."

"Doctorita you should put a hat on her head or she will catch cold."

"Who is the doctor here, you or me?" I wanted to ask. "More likely those kisses you are smothering her with will give her a cold."

"Doctorita you should bind her up from head to foot so that her legs grow strong and straight."

"She likes to wriggle around. She doesn't like anything to restrict her movement," I replied patiently, "and when babies move their muscles lots they grow strong." I was getting fed up of this avalanche of advice. I felt like crying, "If I want your advice I'll ask for it," at the top of my lungs.

"Don't take it to heart so much," Vladimir remonstrated when I complained to him. "Just laugh it off. People feel responsible to look out for every child here. They are just trying to help. Why don't you jot down all the old wives tales you hear and write a book about them one day?"

I laughed, "You are right, but it just feels like they are criticizing me the whole time."

When Tamara started dribbling because her teeth were on the move I found my line of defence against excessive kissing. Seeing her dribble the ladies would laugh and say, "Someone must be kissing your baby on the mouth because she is dribbling a lot." If I asked people not to kiss my baby because they might give her a cold they looked at me as if I were mad. If I asked them not to because she was dribbling too much, they nodded in sage comprehension and did as I asked.

I breast fed freely in public, as was the custom. Women had no qualms about getting their breasts out in public, and indeed if your baby was crying and you did not provide a comforting nipple for them to suck on you received many scandalised looks and pointed stares. One granny was concerned when she saw me breastfeeding in a sleeveless top. She told me I should have my shoulders covered while feeding to keep my milk warm. I thought that was an interesting idea, but quietly ignored her kind advice. Tamara seemed to enjoy my milk regardless of what kind of top I had on. She certainly fed long and frequently. At least it was good for my weight loss plan.

Not so good was Vladimir wanting me to cook fried whole fish, fried bananas and fried chorizo sausage for his breakfast, lunch and tea. "But how am I ever going to lose weight if I have to eat all this grease?" I moaned staring at the fish he had smothered in herbs ready for the frying pan, my heart sinking.

"But this food you eat, diet this and diet that, it isn't real food." He protested.

I sighed to myself and started to cook. "Well I am at least going to boil some broccoli to go with it," I retorted, "You never eat any vegetables."

Vladimir's Granny, arriving to meet her great-granddaughter, was horrified to see her sitting up on my lap. "No, no, my daughter," she remonstrated in kindly tones, "You must not sit her up. It will make her cheeks all saggy." I looked enquiringly at Vladimir who gave me a wink as if to say, "That's one for your book." I'm afraid I carelessly ignored her advice, condemning my daughter to saggy cheeks for life.

Tamara started to hiccup. "She is growing," cried her Great-Granny in delight. "Another one for the book," I giggled to myself. It was becoming quite fascinating.

As I wheeled my shopping trolley through the super-market a perfect stranger touched Tamara's head and firmly exclaimed, "You must put a hat on her head. Every mother knows that." Her tone was most indignant. "And where is her red bracelet?" I felt my defensive bristles rising at this unfair criticism. Vladimir calmly whispered to me not to get upset. "She probably thinks evil spirits, bad air and chills can enter a baby's head through the fontanel. That will be why she is so worried to see Tamara without a hat and protective bracelet. Just don't take any notice."

Even Vladimir was a little anxious about Tamara's tummy button. He went along with me not stuffing it with cotton wool balls and not wrapping a tight cloth around her middle, but watched how her umbilicus developed with an eagle eye. He did not want her to end up with a sticking out tummy button which would render her unable to wear clothes that revealed her mid-rift. That would be too unsightly to be tolerated.

Vladimir and I went together to the market street to buy Tamara her first pair of shoes. It was quite exciting. It felt like a little milestone in our daughter's as yet short life. The lady in the shop was very happy to pass us all the styles she had to try on Tamara, and to offer us some free advice. She told us we should massage her feet with our saliva first thing every morning – she was most emphatic on the importance of the early hour – to prevent her from developing flat feet.

"Why do you have a baby shoe hanging up near the door of the shop?" I asked.

"Why don't you know that finding a lost baby shoe is good luck?" She explained. After that I noticed them all over the place; in shops and hanging from the rear view mirror in taxis. Obviously many babies had kicked off a shoe in their time, and people were only too happy to try and conserve the good luck bestowed upon them in finding them.

Tamara suffered from colic, crying at the same time every afternoon for no apparent reason. I used to walk up and down outside our house singing to her until it passed. Colic drops, aniseed water and gripe water did not honestly seem to make much of a difference. Sonja arrived with some sewing one afternoon while I was pacing up and down with a screaming baby.

When Sonja saw me with Tamara and heard my explanation of what was wrong her eyes lit up. Here was her chance to help me. "My youngest little girl suffered the same problem," she told me excitedly. She leant in close and began to whisper in case anyone overheard us. "My Granny told me a secret remedy for colic. It cured her straight away. Take the kitchen tea towel, when damp from serving the steaming rice from the pot at breakfast time, and touch it to Tamara's mouth three times." She instructed me. "If you follow these instructions precisely I guarantee it will stop the crying." I did not like to tell her I ate toast for breakfast, and that steaming rice pots were not usually found in my kitchen at breakfast time. The colic gradually disappeared in its own good time.

But while I was trying to rise above it all, and laugh instead of take offense, the relentless night after night of broken sleep was taking its toll. "I seem to have lost my sense of humour," I sighed wearily to Vladimir. "I think I am going mad. Everything seems an effort and I just feel like crying all the time."

"What we need is a good night out." Vladimir stated. "Why don't we go to the cinema?"

"Well, that sounds nice," I began, "But who will look after Tamara?"

"Why don't we take her with us?" He asked puzzled. Ecuadorean children stayed up until all hours. They slept when they were tired.

I sighed, "But I am just getting her into a routine of going to bed at eight. At last she is letting me get to bed at a reasonable hour."

"You and your routines! Why can't you be flexible for a change?" He asked annoyed.

"But I need her to get used to going to sleep at eight o'clock. I am so tired. I need to sleep. It is me that has to get up night after night to feed her. You don't even hear her wake up." My eyes were beginning to fill. Vladimir hastily beat a retreat, not wanting to see me cry again.

"OK, OK," he acquiesced, "so what shall we do with Tamara?"

"Why don't we put her to sleep as usual by eight in the evening in her own cot and then go out? We could get a baby sitter."

"That's a novel idea to me, but let's give it a try. I will ask my cousin to come and look after her." Vladimir responded more enthusiastically.

Bemused by the unusual request, but game to help his cousin came and settled into our living room to watch the television while we had our evening out. Our daughter asleep in her bedroom never even knew we had gone. It all worked perfectly, and Vladimir and I came home smiling, having enjoyed the rare treat of a little time alone together.

"Taking care of Tamara is all absorbing, totally exhausting, and utterly fascinating." I commented. "So is being married. It all takes some getting used to."

"You are doing great," Vladimir encouraged me, putting his arms around me. "You are a wonderful Mum."

"I am pleased I have my work in the health centre to go to as well." I remarked, feeling secure in his embrace, "I enjoy the adult conversations and distractions. I also cannot turn a blind eye to the people in need all around me."

"Now I need to get our new business set up." Vladimir said anxiously. "I need to start earning money to look after you both. We can't live off thin air."

In order to be able to stay with us in Santo Domingo Vladimir had decided to grow anthurium flowers to sell in Quito to the florists.

"The plants are doing really well," I encouraged him. "You will soon have flowers to take to sell in the florists."

I was more worried about whether I was doing a good enough job of bringing up Tamara. I was still trying to work out how to look after a baby, and having to defend my way of doing so all the time felt so stressful, and made me doubt myself. "Things will get better as Tamara gets bigger," I told myself, "I know what to do with older children more, and Vladimir and I will know each other better and have found our own way of doing things by then." Feeling unsure of myself I hoped desperately that this was true.

## CHAPTER TWENTY-ONE

# A Catalogue of Accidents

I began to wonder if I was wise bringing up Tamara in Santo Domingo. I was suddenly so much more aware of the dangers and diseases I was exposing her to by being there. It was all very well coming as a single girl to save the world, but now I was responsible for a young baby. I wanted to do the best I could for her.

Road accidents were the third highest cause of death in Ecuador. Vladimir came back week after week from Quito reporting accidents that he had seen on the dangerous hair pin bends. We heard the news that a nineteen year old from the village had come off his motor bike as he whizzed back home one Sunday afternoon. A car driven by a man who had had too much to drink did not see him coming and went straight into him. Carlos had had his helmet slung on his arm, instead of on his head, and had sustained head trauma. He had been taken to the Santo Domingo hospital, who could not do much for him, but as his family were covered by the national insurance scheme, he had been transferred to the hospital in Quito where he had spent several days unconscious in intensive care. He had then made a remarkable recovery and came to see us in the health centre for us to remove stitches from his face. His eye was still black and puffy, and his cheek swollen.

We admonished him to start using his helmet and he nodded his head with a knowing grin, but I do not think I ever saw him wearing it. He went straight back to riding his bike, helmet casually slung over the handlebars.

Darwin, (Vladimir's builder friend who had built the toilets) came in having come off his motorbike as well. He had cut his elbow when he fell and had had it stitched up in the hospital at the weekend. Unfortunately it became infected, and we had to remove the stitches and clean and dress the wound daily until it healed. Darwin had three older sisters who all looked out for him, and made sure he attended for his dressings. They were a very close family, and were all concerned about their little brother. Darwin used to laugh and joke with Monserrat as she attended to him in between grimaces with the pain.

I shuddered as I watched whole families ride on motorbikes, whizzing past our house, baby in arms and toddler sitting up front. They mostly did not bother to put the one helmet they had between them on anyone's head, and were all so vulnerable to injury if they fell off. I had children brought to see me, burns on their legs from touching the exhaust pipe of a motorbike, and young men with macerated skin full of gravel were also frequent customers.

"Your father said he was going to take Tamara on his motorbike today," I reported to Vladmir. "I am telling you now that if I ever see Tamara on one of those death machines I am packing my bags and going back to Scotland. So I hope he was joking."

"Don't exaggerate Andy," Vladimir frowned, "Everyone uses motorbikes here, because they can't afford cars. The majority are fine most of the time."

"Well we have a car and there is no reason to risk my daughter's life and limb by taking her on one of those monstrosities. Look at Darwin, falling off the umpteenth time, or Carlos who almost died. Even your sister has horrible scars from that time she fell off a motorbike. I never ever want to see Tamara on one."

Victor's carer, Janet came with Victor to the health centre. Victor was pale and listless. Janet was very concerned about him. "He is just not himself Doctorita. He had a check-up at the hospital last week, and they did not give him anything different. But he had a seizure two nights ago, and he is just so sleepy and tired. What do you think?"

I examined him carefully and found he was very anaemic. He needed tests to be done to get to the root of his problem. It was sad to see him so down, when he was usually such a happy soul, spreading cheer to all around him. "You need to get him another appointment at the hospital so that they do the tests he needs," I advised. "I can give him this syrup, but we need to find out what is really going on."

"Right," said Janet, "I hope they will give us a quick appointment. It is so hard to obtain them."

"I heard your sad news Janet, how are you doing?" I asked. I had heard her nine year brother had recently lost his life as he tried to get some oranges off a tree using a wet bamboo pole. He touched the electric cables that ran overhead and was electrocuted and died instantly. His whole family were in shock at the tragic death of their only son.

"It is so hard Doctorita," Janet bowed her head in sadness. "The worst is seeing my mother's grief. She simply sits there. She refuses to wash, is losing weight dramatically and just stares and stares at an enlarged photograph of my brother. I don't know how to console her, how to get her to take an interest in life again."

"It will take some time Janet. I cannot imagine what it must be like to lose your son. I will keep praying for you all, and if there is anything I can do, let me know."

"Thank you Doctorita," Janet said quietly as she stood to push Victor back to the orphanage. "I hope we can help little Victor."

I took a moment to myself as Janet left. The death of her brother was such a tragic accident. "It is not that people are deliberately careless." I thought, "A lot of times these accidents are caused by a lack of resources, or a lack of foresight. People don't have the money to buy a car instead of a motorbike, or the means to complain the electricity cables are dangerously low lying. But I think people do just live in the moment as well. They don't think ahead – each day already has enough difficulties of its own to be faced. I think people struggle so much for daily existence, that they are simply resigned to accepting whatever life throws at them. Even Vladimir does not worry about safety as much as I do."

We went out in the car together and I strapped Tamara firmly into her car seat. A little way down the road she started to cry, wanting to get out of the car seat and sit on my lap. "Aww, let her out of the seat," Vladimir pleaded, "I don't like to hear her cry like that."

"But it is better she is in the seat so she is safe if you have to brake suddenly or have a crash. I don't want her to fly through the windscreen." I replied.

"You are so cold hearted." Vladimir retorted, "How can you bear to hear her cry like that?"

"You are so sentimental." I complained. "It is better she is safe and unhappy than that she is unsafe and happy."

"Nothing is going to happen. Get her out of the seat, Andy..."

I went out and bought some chicken wire and sticks to make a gate for the steps leading up to the roof of our house.

"Why are you making the gate before she can even walk?" Vladimir asked, amused at my forward thinking.

"You would wait until you saw her going up the steps before you made a gate." I retorted.

"You want to plan everything so much in advance. There is enough to think about today, without worrying about the future."

"But she will be walking before you know it, and it is better to have the gate up before she does. I don't want her falling down the steps."

We were still debating the point when Janet came to our gate with Victor. He had suffered another seizure. "Doctorita, it was so long this time. I thought it was never going to stop. Is there anything you can give him?"

I looked at poor little Victor, asleep in the pushchair and wished there were more I could do. "Have you got an appointment at the hospital yet?"

"He has one for a month's time, but they do not want to change it for any sooner."

"He really needs to see his specialist," I lamented. "If he starts seizing again give him this medicine to stop the seizure, but keep trying to get him seen in the hospital." I advised.

"It is so difficult here if you have a severe illness," I commented to Vladimir once they had gone. "Victor's case is so complicated he really needs a specialist review, but it is so hard to get an appointment quickly. He is really sick."

"I think the health service in Britain is amazing." Vladimir remarked, "Here the whole thing is a lottery and mostly the attention you receive depends on how much you can pay."

"What would we do if Tamara became seriously ill? The lack of good health services does make me nervous about living here."

"She won't get ill. She is healthy." Vladimir shrugged it off.

"But you never know what might happen," I insisted. "What if she did get sick?"

"We will cope with that if it happens. I don't think it is a big enough risk for us to go and live in Scotland now just in case though, do you?"

"Well, no, I don't think so. I suppose it is unlikely." I had to agree, still worried.

We went off to bed, sleeping like logs until the 'phone rang relentlessly dragging us back to consciousness. "Doctorita, please can you come to the orphanage, Victor is very unwell."

He died before I got there.

Vladimir, Tamara and I all went to his funeral, a simple ceremony held in the Orphaids chapel, celebrating his life and the joy he had given to so many during his short time with us. He had always had a smile for those who greeted him.

Then we took his coffin in the back of the pick up to the nearby graveyard, and the pastor led the singing of a simple hymn and Bible reading as we said our good byes to little Victor. All the staff and children watched as the men present took turns in filling in his grave. We placed some flowers on the mound of earth and the children from the orphanage carefully placed tributes they had prepared for Victor.

We gathered by the cars to share a coke and biscuits together before heading home. Victor was a special little boy who would always be remembered in many hearts. I pictured him now able to run and talk in heaven, filling the air with his beautiful laugh. I felt joy in my heart that he had gone to be with his Heavenly Father and was now whole. But he would be missed, and I could not help thinking that had he been born in a different country he would have lived a little longer. I turned to Jesus who saw all the injustices in the world and placed my hope in Him again, that one day all our tears would be wiped away.

## CHAPTER TWENTY-TWO

# Project Ecuador

I was going through a period of great adjustment. I had gone from being young free and single to married with baby in such a short space of time. I was permanently exhausted and struggling to cope with the demands of a young baby in a culture so different to my own upbringing. I still desperately wanted to serve the people of Ecuador, to help the sick and needy on my doorstep, but worried I was compromising Tamara's care in doing so. Vladimir did his best to understand and help, but simply did not really know where I was coming from half the time, or why I worried about things that to him were normal. I did not regret having married him and I loved my baby to bits. But it was hard work. Life suddenly seemed to have become much more complicated.

I also felt isolated from life back home; sad that my siblings could no longer see their niece, and that Tamara had forgotten her Granny who loved her so much. Friendships that had been important to me before had inevitably waned as distance and time took their toll. I felt that I no longer belonged in Britain, but that I did not completely fit in Ecuador either. I had to rely on Vladimir almost exclusively for support and company, whereas he had a wide support base of family and friends right on his doorstep. I feared I made him feel confined and restrained, that he was secretly longing to be free again.

My sister Rachel's arrival to visit us accompanied by her friend Karen was a gift from God. They filled the house with their laughter and fun, enjoyed playing with Tamara, made me endless cups of coffee, and brought with them a much needed energy boost in the form of Cadbury's chocolate. Most importantly they brought a refreshing perspective on life.

It was interesting driving them around and hearing their comments about what they saw. Their reactions and exclamations helped Vladimir to see that I was not alone in the way I viewed life in Santo Domingo. They were horrified to see cars driving around with shattered windscreens, apparently unconcerned. They thought the spikes the lorry drivers liked to attach to their wheels were a menace, and exclaimed at the clouds of black smoke that were puffed out of some buses making their way around town, filling the air with pollution.

Rachel thought the most attractive features of Santo Domingo were the roundabouts. There were several impressive ones to be seen; a statue of Colorado Indians, a statue of the Independence winning hero Simon Bolivar, and a revolving globe with fountains elegantly showering water all around it were all on display. It was just a shame the rest of the town with its chaos, dirt and muddle did not match up. I was amused to see photos of these very roundabouts on the Santo Domingo page of a tourist magazine of Ecuador some time later. Rachel was right; they were its most presentable feature.

They loved Vladimir, ever the tour guide, showing them the bananas growing on their plants, the cocoa beans in their pods, and the pineapples growing in the fields nearby. He made them have a go at mounting a donkey that was used for carrying bananas and pointed out the iguanas sunbathing on a sunny afternoon. They jumped in the back of the pick-up truck to find out what riding out back was like, and were shocked by the sight of entire families piled onto motorbikes. They were exhausted by the heat, even though they had come at the cooler time of year, and were mercilessly bitten around the ankles by the midges, despite lashings of insect repellent.

I was pleased to have the chance for a heart-to-heart with my sister. "It is so hard looking after a baby," I confided, "I am just exhausted the whole time, and I wonder if I am doing it right. I haven't got Mum on hand to ask. People here criticize me the whole time; I think they think I am crazy, that my way of doing things is very odd. Even Vladimir thinks I am too inflexible about her routine and bedtime."

"Tamara seems a very happy, secure baby to me," my sister encouraged me. "I think you are doing a wonderful job. Just keep on doing what you think best, never mind what other people think. And you have to take into account that Vladimir must have had a very different upbringing to us."

"I do worry if I spend too much time working, if I should spend more time with Tamara."

"But you spend loads of time with her. I think you are managing to mix work and baby well. You can even take her with you to work. You can't do that in Britain." Rachel reminded me.

"Maybe I shouldn't worry so much." I laughed, "It just seems such a responsibility, having a baby to look after, and I want to do the best job possible. I wonder if she will be happy and safe growing up in Ecuador, or if we should go back to Britain. But then Vladimir would be unhappy. He loves living here."

As I listened to myself I realised I had forgotten to trust in God. He had given me my precious daughter. He had given me Vladimir. He had brought me to Ecuador. While we believed our work for Him was still here, in Santo Domingo, I had to trust Him for our daily needs and protection. Worry was only making me uptight and anxious. I asked for His peace to flood my soul once again.

Vladimir's brother Frank arrived from Spain to visit while Rachel was still with us, so his family decided to literally kill the fattened pig in celebration. Vladimir's Mum was formidable with her butcher's knife, directing proceedings as they slaughtered the pig and set about preparing every part of its body for the feast.

The slaughtered, bled pig was heaved up on to a couple of poles and paraded ceremonially on the shoulders of some of the men to the cooking area to be chopped up for the pot. Every part of the animal was put to use.

The skin and fat was cut up and fried, the bucket of greasy crackling eagerly passed around the many members of the family gathering. This stomach churning delicacy was a definite favourite that I politely declined. I was still receiving too many "You look so lovely and fat" comments for my liking.

The intestines were cleaned and filled with a minced up mish-mash of the offal. This was made into sausages. The meat was cut up on the bone and fried in huge pans over charcoal fires, having been plastered in a mixture of salt, garlic, and cumin. Manioc and maize were boiled in vast quantities to accompany the meat, with a salad of finely sliced red onion and tomato marinated in lime juice and salt.

Most of Vladimir's family were there; the many Aunts, Uncles, cousins and second cousins, his Granny, parents and sister. Tamara was whisked off and I did not see her again until she started to cry for some milk. The women busied themselves over the fires, stirring and tossing, and mingled amongst the throng constantly offering food to all. The men divided themselves into two teams and started a football match in the field where Great-Granny's horses fed. We settled down to watch the contest, which was played out with great seriousness and shouts of laughter.

Finally everyone ended up in the river cooling off after all the exercise, splashing and rubbing themselves all over with soap. Tamara enjoyed a splash about with us as well, accustomed as she was to the chill of the water. It was beautiful to bathe under the shade of the bamboo branches that hung languidly over the water. Little fish nipped and darted between our legs, tickling us gently as they passed. Further downstream we could see white storks posing elegantly on one leg as they rested on the rocks. It was great to see everyone enjoying themselves together, making the most of this special time together as a family.

"Vladimir has a lovely family," Rachel commented, impressed by their warmth and hospitality. "They certainly know how to put on a feast and it is so good to see them all enjoying themselves like that."

"I think that is one of the things I most appreciate about being here in Ecuador, the close family and community spirit. They are always ready to lend a helping hand."

"It is really special," Rachel agreed. "I think Tamara will love growing up here. You should relax and enjoy the experience."

Rachel and Karen came with me some mornings to the health centre to babysit Tamara and see what we got up to there. They played with the children in the waiting room, and met some of our regular customers.

"Why are some of these children not at school?" Rachel quizzed me, as she played ball with them.

"Their parents cannot afford to send them," I explained. "At the start of each school year these children need shoes, uniform, exercise books, pens and pencils, art materials and books. During the year they also need bus fares, toilet paper and drinking water for their school. People around here live from hand to mouth. They do not have any extra money to pay for these things, so their children do not go to school."

"That is awful," Rachel and Karen were shocked. "Every child should have the opportunity to go to school. We are going to do something about this."

And so the charity Project Ecuador was born.

Once back home Rachel and Karen set about finding sponsors to help children to be able to go to school, and set up the charity Project Ecuador to run this and the other projects I was involved in. Their enthusiasm and energy gave me a much needed boost. I felt I suddenly had much more support behind me for the work I was doing. I felt that they believed in me and that what I was doing was important. I knew I had people behind me praying for me. I felt much more connected with home again.

Vladimir was pleased to be able to contribute to the charity work now and he set about helping me select the first children to be sponsored with enthusiasm. Genesis was a ten year old girl with about seven brothers. She was often seen wearing boy's clothes as her parents rarely had the money to buy her pretty things and she had to wear her brothers' hand-me-downs. They lived in a tiny wooden house precariously balanced on stilts. It was a great help to the whole family to have a sponsor: not only did it enable Genesis to have all she needed to attend the local Primary school, but it enabled her parents to be able to afford to send her younger brothers.

"We should put Anderson on the list," Vladimir volunteered, "He is also from a large family and lives in a similarly ramshackle wooden house. Tell the sponsors that he loves football, and is always to be seen kicking a ball around with his mates of an afternoon, when he is not helping his father to cut bananas. Hopefully if we find him a sponsor he will continue on to secondary school next year instead of leaving school aged eleven as his older brothers have done."

"Little Mischief", nicknamed for his endless pranks, was an eight year old who lived with his Grandfather. "Should we put him on the list?" I asked Vladimir.

"Oh definitely, his mother has four children all with different fathers, and she herself looks after none of them. Little Mischief struggles at school as there is no one at home to help explain things to him when he does not understand them. His Grandfather is illiterate." Vladimir elaborated.

They lived in a falling down cane house on stilts. His Grandfather, though getting on in years, still worked in the fields to feed them both. Having a sponsor enabled them to buy all the materials Little Mischief needed for school so that he could take part in all the classes and activities. Previously he had lacked plimsolls to join in physical education, paints and paper to join in art classes, and books from which to study maths and Spanish.

"This is great," I enthused to Vladimir, "This is going to make such a difference in these kids' lives."

"They will feel so special having someone take an interest in them, and if they get a present, wow they will be so excited! Let's hope they really make the most of this opportunity and make something of themselves."

We went to a neighbouring village to ask the teacher there, Erika, if she had any children in her school needing a sponsor. She nearly cried with happiness to think of some of her children being able to benefit from such a scheme. "I have these two nine year old girls who desperately need help," she told us, pointing them out. They were not in uniform because they had not been able to afford to buy it. "Jennifer is one of five children, and her mother is expecting a sixth. They are all close together in age and live squashed together in a tiny house on a small plot of land where her parents grow a few bananas. They are very poor. Karla also comes from a large family, living in similar circumstances. She often misses school because of illness caused by poor nutrition. Her parents do not have the money to buy their family good food. When we were donated some powered milk for the children Karla was so hungry she immediately went to the bathroom to mix some up with the water there to drink."

"It will be a great pleasure to help them," we assured her, shocked by Karla's tale. "Here let me jot down their stories. Now we need to take a photo of them both to send to the potential sponsors. As soon as we hear any news we will come and tell you."

"It is such a great help to these families," Vladimir smiled, "I wish we could do it for all the villages round here."

"It is such a good way to help people isn't it? Education is fundamental to giving them the chance to make something of themselves in life, to be able to find the route out of poverty." I was delighted we were able to do this work together.

Rachel asked me to find out when the children had their birthdays, as some of the sponsors were asking. It proved to be an interesting exercise. Señora Maria, mother of Araceli, had trouble remembering her children's birthdays, first because she had so many children, and second because they had made them up when they finally got round to registering them. When she reached the birthday of Gabriela, her youngest, I realised it was her birthday that very day. "Why Señora Maria it is Gabriela's birthday today!" I exclaimed in excitement.

Señora Maria simply said, "Why so it is! Happy birthday Gabriela!" And that was the sum total of Gabriela's birthday celebration that year. They did not normally remember them at all.

When I asked Karla's mother when her birthday was she screwed up her face in puzzlement and tried hard to remember. After a few seconds she said, "Well I am pretty sure she was born in August. Put down the nineteenth, that's close enough."

When I asked Genesis when her birthday was, she said she did not know but would ask her mother. A little while later she was back at my gate excited to tell me that her mother had said it was her birthday the following Saturday. She wondered if her sponsor was going to send her a gift. I did not have the heart to explain that even if her sponsor posted something that very day it would not arrive by Saturday, so I just told her to come back on Saturday to see.

Saturday dawned and I baked a cake for her and wrapped up some little trinkets I had found for her. Sure enough, after lunch a little face appeared at the gate anxious to see if there was any gift. When I presented her with the cake and present she flushed pink in excitement and anticipation, and waving her thanks and delight ran off down the road home to show off her gifts. I do not suppose she had ever had a birthday cake before. That was her eleventh birthday.

Vladimir and I stood hand in hand and shared a smile as we watched her go happily on her way. "This is why we are in Ecuador," I grinned. "Today we made one little girl very happy."

# CHAPTER TWENTY-THREE

# Monsters and Rag Dolls

The creation of Project Ecuador gave new impetus to the work in Ecuador. Rachel, Karen and many others did an amazing job of finding sponsors, raising funds, selling crafts and providing inspiration.

That Christmas my dream of giving each child in the village a Christmas present, came true. The UK team raised the funds. I set the sewing group the task of making the presents and of course paid them for their wares. This had the added benefits of giving the local women the work, and also providing a good quality present for the children.

We set about making rag dolls for the girls and felt monsters for the boys. We donated sewing machines to the sewing families. They did have some experience of sewing machines, but now they had the opportunity to practice a lot more and improve their skills. We spent some afternoons at my house going over how to use and look after the machines, and then they took them home and started making dolls.

The first attempts were not always symmetrical or evenly sewn, but very quickly the quality became ever better, and more importantly the girls were growing in self-confidence and were proud of their newly acquired skills. We had been donated a sack full of scraps of materials, ideal for making the dolls with. Each one had a unique combination of clothing and colours, and we made them with bright pink, yellow and red wool for their hair. The girls enjoyed plaiting the hair, and attaching pretty ribbons, sequins and flowers to the dolls as finishing touches. They became works of art. They were made with love.

Those who were not yet ready to tackle sewing machines I gave the task of hand-sewing the monsters. They had a field day choosing all kinds of combinations of bright colours to make them with, and stitched their funny faces with great aplomb. The results were great; bold and cheeky monsters galore. We looked forward to giving them out to the boys at Christmas.

In the end we had enough funds to make three hundred toys. We donated a hundred to the Life in Abundance Trust. They gave them to the very poor children who came to their church project in a slum area of Santo Domingo. It was an impoverished place, built on top of a disused rubbish dump, filled with small children suffering from malnutrition and disease. The charity workers were enchanted by the cute toys. They were delighted to be able to brighten the children's Christmas with them.

The rest we gave out in the village at that year's Christmas party. After the party games and the plate of food, the children sat in circles on the ground ready for the giving of the presents. They received them with such delight and happiness. The place was full of smiles and giggles. They were the only gift many of those children received that year. For many months to come I would see little girls clutching dolls they had been given as they wandered around the village, or spot a monster sitting on a bed when I went to visit a patient. It brought a huge smile to my face every time.

The sponsored children also received a Christmas present. Genesis was delighted to receive a parcel full of girls' clothes; pretty skirts and sparkly tops, she was in heaven. I took a photo of her wide grin to send back to her sponsor.

I began visiting some of the local schools with toothbrushes for the children, worm medicine and Christian story books for them to read. The teachers were very open and always pointed out how the sponsored children were doing and gave me copies of their reports at the end of term to send to their sponsors. The children would run up and hug me as I arrived; delighted someone was taking an interest in them. "Doctorita, Doctorita," they would cry, as they held on to whatever part of me they could reach, "What are we going to do today? Is that your baby? Can I hold her?" I hugged and kissed them back and gave them each a little attention. I felt honoured to be the person who could reach out and touch them and give them God's blessing.

It was an aside comment that started the priceless adventure of providing spectacles for the school children. The observation that one never saw children in

Ecuador wearing glasses brought me up short. It was so obvious I had not seen it staring me in the face. There must be children who could not see well all around me who could be helped so easily. What a difference it could make to them.

Funds came in for Operation Vision through the running of a half-marathon, and I set to work. I took two health promoters with me to the schools and screened all the children using a simple Snellen chart. Those we were not satisfied could see all the letters we selected to take into town on a subsequent day to the optician.

The children and parents piled into the pickup, happily sitting out in the back as well as in the cab. A little girl riding up front so seldom left her village that she asked me if we were going to a different country. It was all a huge adventure to her.

When we arrived at the optician the children gasped in amazement at the pretty sight of the sparkling lights reflecting in rows and rows of spectacles. They could not wait to get started and find out if they were going to receive a pair.

The optician did a more thorough sight test on each of the children. Many of them did need glasses. Julia and her cousin Anna were severely short sighted and had lazy eyes. They were aged eight and nine, and still could not read the alphabet, because they could not see it clearly enough. Julia's mother exclaimed, "All this time I have been buying vitamin syrups to try and improve Julia's brain. I could not understand why she was not learning.

I used to tell her off for not paying attention in class and thought she was stupid. Finally I know the reason why and we can do something about it. Thank you so much. This is going to transform her life."

These two girls were delighted to try out the frames and choose pink ones that they liked. They understood they would have to wear them all day every day, and their Mums promised to take them back for regular reviews, which the optician offered to do without charge. What a difference these spectacles were going to make to these girls. Not only did it enable them to start learning, it also boosted their self-confidence. No longer were they considered stupid or lazy. They blossomed as they showed what they were truly capable of now their disability had been discovered.

Jessica was thirteen and soon to be finishing primary school. She had a stigmatism. She loved her glasses and the difference they made to her vision. She was determined to go on to study Secondary School now that it was to be much easier for her.

Steven received a pair of glasses and went from being bottom of the class to achieving a place in the top three. Neither his Grandmother nor his teachers had suspected he could not see properly.

An old man in the optician at the same time as us grumblingly asked why we had brought in children, when it was only old people who needed spectacles. When I went to the schools with the finished spectacles and the children tried them on for the first time the other children in the class called them "Granny" or "Grandpa". I suppose they had simply never seen young people wearing glasses. It made me giggle.

Their teachers and I led the way in calling them professional looking, budding engineers, doctors and teachers. Most of the children wore their glasses without apology, appreciating the great difference it made to them, and paying no attention to the teasing that others soon forgot about anyway as they became accustomed to seeing their classmates with specs.

I was encouraged to see the children we gave glasses to wearing them when we went back to visit the schools on other occasions. It was such an exciting way to be able to help these children. And there were still other schools to be visited and children to be assisted in this way.

I gave of my time willingly, gladly, lovingly when I went out to the health centre, the schools or on visits. But in afternoons that I was home with Tamara, wanting to dedicate my time and attention to her I resented the constant interruptions and intrusions. Being a mother was very important to me and I thought that Tamara needed my undivided attention as well. The demands of others for my time caused me much inner conflict: I was loath to turn them away, but my mother's heart cried out against having my precious hours with my daughter stolen from me.

I did not mind the sewing group coming round on the ordained days, as the children played with Tamara and gave her company which she loved. They were friends. I did not even mind the children with sponsors popping in, asking for money for things they needed for school, bringing me receipts once they had spent the money, and bringing copies of their school reports at the end of each term. They were quickly attended to and also liked to play with and entertain Tamara. It was good to hear how they were progressing at school.

But I did not like patients coming looking for me at home. I did my best to encourage them to go and see me in the health centre in the mornings, and deliberately did not have many medicines at home to give to people. Having the children pop by was one thing, even attending the occasional real emergency, but starting to examine routine patients demanded my time and attention, and Tamara would inevitably start screaming, needing me as well. I did not think it was fair on her for me to carry on working at home, and came to resent these intrusions.

I also feared letting strangers in. Robberies were common. Every so often Vladimir came home with news of robberies that had taken place; a neighbour had their motorbike stolen at gunpoint, Little Mischief's Grandfather had his gas cylinder stolen one Sunday afternoon while he was watching the local football team play, and a neighbouring house left unoccupied for a night was stripped of its contents. Vladimir always left in the morning telling me to keep the gate locked and only let in people that we knew.

Some of the patients who came to our gate could be very insistent, even rudely so, determined that their need to be seen in the afternoon when it was convenient to them was more important that my reasons for requesting they go to the health centre the next morning. "Doctorita, my neighbour told me to come here. They told me you could help me, that you are a wonderful doctor. I have to work tomorrow morning, so I cannot go to the health centre. I need you to attend me now."

"But I do not have anything here to examine you with or to prescribe you medicines." I remonstrated. "I am looking after my baby at the moment. I have to ask you to come to the health centre one morning when I can attend you properly."

"Don't be a bad person," the patient insisted. "Come with us and open the health centre now. We are busy in the mornings."

"Then I am sorry but you will have to find a different doctor if you cannot come and see me one morning." I stuck to my guns, feeling guilty for not opening my gate and helping them there and then, but also resenting their expectation that I would do so. I was only willing to help them on my terms, not theirs.

Sometimes I simply did not go to the gate when people called, but hid away in the house, determined to have time alone with my little one. It was easier that way. Sometimes I was making the most of Tamara having a nap by enjoying one myself, and never even heard the knocks and cries of "Doctorita, Doctorita".

I wanted to help everyone who asked, I was sure Jesus never turned anyone away. But I was unable to do likewise. People thought I was brave for living in Ecuador, strong and capable, full of faith. But I knew it was not true. I was just a weak human being, full of faults, self-doubts and selfishness. I let God and others down. But the God I knew was my loving Heavenly Father, and He cheered me on graciously, despite my stumbling efforts. He promised not to blow out the flickering candle, but to fan it into flame again. The work was His.

## CHAPTER TWENTY-FOUR

# When in Rome Do as the Romans Do

Things seemed to become increasingly difficult. One day I woke up and was horrified to look in the mirror and find that I had fallen victim to the dreaded "Chinese foot" disease that was running riot in the village.

I do not know why the disease had this name. It was a form of conjunctivitis, I presume viral, that used to come in epidemics. Suddenly lots of people were walking around wearing sunglasses so you could not see their puffy eyes.

My eyes were grossly swollen, oozing pus, bright red and hurt like crazy. It was real pain in the eyes, not just an annoying scratchy sensation that I had experienced in previous milder episodes of conjunctivitis. I looked like a monster.

Vladimir refused to come anywhere near me for days, scared I was going to pass it to him. This technique seemed to work, as he never came down with it. Tamara did develop it as well, but in a much milder form.

As is often the case when a disease is self-limiting there were many recommended treatments. I was told to wash my eyes with fizzy water, with chamomile tea, and with Aloe Vera. Some people bought antibiotic eye ointments, but those who did not got better just the same. Other people recommended applying drops of breast milk to my eyes or banana leaves cooled in the fridge.

Tamara woke in the night with a high fever. She had tell-tale white spots in her mouth and a couple of days later started with a rash on her face that spread to the rest of her body. Still too young to be vaccinated for the measles she had caught the virus. I felt very guilty for exposing her to it and it broke my heart to see her crying from the fevers day after day.

None of us got much sleep that week as Tamara fought off the illness, thankfully with no long term ill effects. The worst night we were up trying to distract her at three in the morning, while she was delirious with fever, manically trying to play with her toys at top speed. Thankfully after that she turned the corner and rapidly began to improve. When she was finally getting better I took her to Vladimir's Mum for a morning and sank thankfully into the oblivion of a desperately needed deep sleep.

I then faced a seemingly insurmountable mound of paperwork that needed to be done. This was what I hated most in Ecuador; the days and days required to obtain the permits and papers required. "I am losing the will to live," I groaned to Vladimir one morning, "I have so much paperwork to get sorted. It is horrendous. It robs me of precious hours I could be spending with Tamara."

"You will get it done," Vladimir stated matter of fact. "It is just how things are." He did not understand why I made such a fuss about it all. It was perfectly normal to him.

I had to renew the permit for the health centre, which involved trips to the fire station, the local government office, the bank, and inspectors coming. They told me the law had changed and I could no longer stock medicines in the health centre. Patients would have to go to a pharmacy in town to buy them. I sighed heartily; another obstacle to overcome.

I had to renew my permit to prescribe psychotropic drugs. This involved registering with the new association of doctors in Santo Domingo, trips to several offices and banks. I stood in the queues imagining all the things I could have been doing to use my time better. I could have been treating the sick, visiting schools, or simply helping Tamara take her first faltering steps. I detested my precious time being stolen from me in this manner.

Then I had to renew my car registration. This was my worst bugbear; the police station was the worst organised place in Santo Domingo. The first time I went a fight broke out among unsatisfied customers, and I beat a hasty retreat. After queuing up at five in the morning for several more days I managed to finally obtain my needed registration, only to realise my driving licence was about to run out and I was going to have to go back again to the dreaded police station. Why they could not organise an appointment system I did not know. Why they had to ask for so many pointless photocopies of equally pointless documents I did not know. What were they going to do with them all for goodness sake? I was sure they just invented papers to waste a bit more precious time.

My heart sinking, I also had to renew my identity card and census card, which meant going for entire days to Quito and spending hours waiting in queues. I was coming to the end of my tether. I had to leave Tamara with my mother-in-law so much, and resented every hour taken from me by the endless trips to utterly inefficient offices for papers I wished heartily I could live without. I wanted to be the one bringing up my daughter. I did not want to have to leave her so much, not even with Vladimir's Mum.

Tired and stressed I cried at the least little thing, and saw spectres where they were none in reality. Vladimir became annoyed at my tears as he felt helpless to know what to do to stop them. I convinced myself he had only married me because he wanted to father Tamara, and felt more isolated and sad than ever. Tamara seemed to love her time with her Abuela (Granny), and ironically this made me feel even worse. I felt even my own daughter loved her Abuela more than she did me. Feeling bad about myself, I treated those around me brusquely and abruptly, forgetting my Ecuadorean manners, and hurting others without realising I was doing so.

"I do not like how much your parents spoil Tamara," I complained to Vladimir testily, "They give her far too many sweets and if she cries they give her anything she wants."

"They are her grandparents." Vladimir defended them, "You should be grateful they help us out so much in looking after her."

"But I want to bring up my own daughter my own way. I don't like how people bring up children here. There is no discipline or routine."

"You are very proud." Vladimir's comment brought me up short.

"What do you mean?" I enquired, taken aback.

"You are proud of your culture. You think that everything British is better than everything Ecuadorean; the ways you do daily business, the ways you bring up children, the food you eat. You do not greet the health promoters with a kiss when you arrive at work and speak rudely to people and expect them to take it because you are white. Why are you in Ecuador if you do not like anything about it?"

His observations hit home. In my fear that I was going to do a bad job of caring for Tamara I had lost sight of all I loved and appreciated about this adopted country of mine. I had forgotten I was the guest here, and had expected people to make allowances for me, when it should have been the other way around. My own insecurities had made me jealous of his mother, when she was going out of her way to be helpful to us. There was no point me being there if I was not going to live graciously in love. I realised I needed to start compromising.

So I made an effort to "while in Ecuador, do as the Ecuadoreans do." I made sure I greeted and took my leave of everyone with a kiss on the cheek, and found I received many more smiles in response. I let Tamara stay up when there was a family gathering so we could join in with the rest for longer. Vladimir relaxed in relief. I tried not to worry when I left Tamara with her Abuela, held my tongue about the sweets and just brushed her teeth thoroughly when I took her home again. "After all they did a good job bringing up Vladimir," I told myself, "I should trust them with their granddaughter."

I realised it was me who had to make the effort to understand and appreciate the people around me and the way they lived. They had never been to the UK. They did not have a clue what life was like there. They were not ever going to understand me. It was pointless of me to expect it.

I realised there was good and bad in both our cultures. I learned to celebrate the good of both in the privacy of our home. I was a world citizen, a citizen of God's world. This world was not my home, I was just passing through. I was never going to feel completely at home and comfortable with everything whether I was living in Britain or in Ecuador. But I could love and appreciate the people around me; people just like me, whom God had created equal, people who wanted to be loved. People who needed to know His love.

Yet despite my best efforts to behave better I still could not stop crying in private, at the least little thing.

A lawyer friend at church took me aside and told me one of the ladies in the sewing group had been to see her to ask if she could sue me for not paying her the minimum wage. The lawyer told me she had given her short thrift, informing her she had completely misunderstood our relationship: I was buying her products, not giving her employment. The lawyer was outraged at the lady's ingratitude. I was saddened because I had thought she was a friend. I felt like I had been stabbed in the back and it hurt like crazy.

The mother of a sponsored child invited me to lunch, which I very much enjoyed with the family's warm welcome and friendly chatter. I thought it was simply a thank you lunch, a gesture of friendship.

Then as I turned to go the mother took me aside and asked me if I could give her money to build a better house. I understood where she was coming from, I really did. She was desperate to improve her circumstances, of course she was. But I also felt like I did not have a true friend in Ecuador. Those who were good to me only did so because they thought they would get some money out of me. It felt very lonely.

Vladimir came home to find me crying again and imme-diately went outside to go and swing in the hammock. I followed him a few minutes later and sat beside him.

"Are you depressed Andy?" He asked concerned.

"No," I replied, "I am just tired; tired and stressed out. Everything has happened so fast it takes a lot of getting used to that's all."

He looked me in the eyes gently and stated, "I just want to you be happy. I hate seeing you cry."

The world stood still for a moment as that simple statement resonated in my heart. He wanted me to be happy. He loved me. I did not have to try so hard. He loved me.

"So you did not marry me just because I was expecting your baby?" I asked, looking up at his kind face.

"Of course not. I love you and I cannot stand seeing you so unhappy. Do you want to go and live in Britain?"

Joy flooded my soul as I knew I was loved. I was loved. And I heard God's whisper, "I love you most of all, my precious daughter," and knew that all the wonderful gifts I received came from Him. I knew with great certainty that I did not want to go and live in Britain. I knew there was still work for me to do in Ecuador; patients to be cured, children to be helped, people to be loved. I knew I was not doing it on my own. God had given me family, and was with me every step of the way.

## CHAPTER TWENTY-FIVE

# Thank you

I began to see tokens of God's love, little messages from Him to me everywhere, rainbow promises of His constancy.

There was a woman banging persistently on my gate at seven in the morning. Vladimir had already left for work and I was alone trying to feed and dress Tamara. I tried to ignore the woman, but she saw me through the window and banged and yelled all the louder trying to attract my attention. Eventually I gave in and slowly, reluctantly, walked out to the gate to find out what help she was wanting from me.

As I approached the gate, Tamara sat on my hip, I realised it was the daughter of a patient of mine. The patient was an old lady who had diabetes who had developed a sacral pressure sore after being in hospital in a diabetic coma for a few days. When she had first come to see us she had been weak, wheelchair bound and despondent. With wound dressings, tender loving care and plenty of encouragement for her anxious family she now had a healed ulcer and was back on her feet, cooking and looking after her family. It had been a pleasure looking after her. She had been so thoroughly delighted to be back to her usual daily chores. It had been wonderful to see her smiling in joy and thankfulness to God for her healing.

I wondered what her daughter wanted and why she had not waited to see me in the health centre. I was planning how I could politely ask her to go to the health centre when she greeted me and produced a beautiful pink frilly dress for a little girl. She told me her sister was a dress maker, and that they were so grateful for the help their mother had received they wanted to give me the dress for my daughter. For a moment I was so taken aback I was speechless. Then I recovered my wits and thanked her profusely for the pretty and totally unexpected gift. It made my day. Tamara felt like a princess wearing it. I walked on air.

There must have been thankfulness in the air, because that Saturday at lunchtime another patient turned up at my gate. She had had a venous leg ulcer, which had healed after several months of frequent dressings. We had got to know her well over the months and counted her a friend. She was over the moon to be well again, out and about her business, so she had found it in her heart to bring us a cooked guinea pig for our lunch, complete with potatoes and a chilli peanut sauce. Vladimir was drooling with anticipation: guinea pig was one of his favourite meals. Even I tucked in with enthusiasm having grown to appreciate this delicacy. "Look, I am really Ecuadorean now!" I joked as we ate. I felt aglow at being appreciated. The world looked a brighter place again.

Next to knock at the gate was the father of a little girl who had a sponsor to help her go to school. They lived in a village some forty five minutes away into the countryside and were very poor, living off the land and staying in a caretaker cottage on a farm. His daughter Anna was doing very well at school, getting top marks. The whole family was very thankful for the help they received to buy Anna her books and uniform for school. Her father had come with a sack containing two live chickens. He explained one was for me and that the other was for the lady who sponsored Anna.

I did not think customs officials would allow us to send the second chicken to the dear lady in question, so both chickens duly ended up in our cooking pot. They made delicious soups, and more importantly continued the replenishing of my stores of energy and goodwill. God was bathing me in His love and I let it spill out to those around me.

Tamara finally began to allow me the long forgotten luxury of a whole uninterrupted night's sleep and the jaded scales of exhaustion began to fall from my eyes. I started to see the world with more equanimity once again.

Problems no longer appeared so mountainous. I found again the capacity to make allowances for my own and other people's faults. I was able to enjoy the people I spent time with for who they were, not asking more of them than they were able to give. I stopped craving toast and tea and was able to enjoy prawn ceviche for breakfast, and green banana turnovers stuffed with meat for supper.

I stopped trying to achieve all my goals by yesterday and being frustrated by missed deadlines. Things took the time they took, and no amount of stressing about them would make any difference. I learnt to use that common Ecuadorian expression, "Mañana." (Tomorrow)

I embraced the spontaneity of life in Ecuador. I did not make plans that were inevitably going to be frustrated, but lived a day at a time, making the most of the opportunities each day brought along.

I redoubled my effort that when in Ecuador one should live as the Ecuadoreans do (at least outside my own home). If I could not face eating a meal I embraced the doggy bag tradition and took it home for Vladimir to eat, without causing any offence to the host. I joined in giving advice to those I had a gem to offer, even when I was not asked, to demonstrate my concern. I listened with interest to all the advice I was given and had a private laugh about the more absurd offerings in the sanctity of my own home.

I took more time to enjoy the visitors that came our way, no matter what their intentions or requests. Alicia dropped by from time to time. I would ask about her paralysed husband Jeovhanny, and her daughters' progress through secondary school, and she would bring me milk from her cows and eggs from her chickens.

One day she gave me a cutting from a tree that produced beautiful white flowers in the morning. By the evening time the flowers changed in colour to a deep fuchsia pink. I was delighted when the cutting took and produced a similar tree in our garden. It was a marvellous, soul reviving gift.

Vladimir helped her sell her pink anthurium flowers by taking them to Quito for her with the flowers he grew, and she brought us some fruits I had never seen before. They had prickly skin, and hard, white, sweet flesh which crunched delightfully in the mouth. I planted the stones from the middle, according to Alicia's instructions and grew several trees which I hoped would produce fruit one day.

At Christmas time she brought photos of her daughters and a card thanking me for helping to pay for their schooling. I sent them to their sponsors to thank them for giving this amazing gift to those young ladies.

Through her quiet offerings she made me feel her appreciation for all the help we gave her family, and it made me glad we could continue to help her.

Her older daughter Maricela, now aged twenty, invited me to her secondary school graduation ceremony. She was proud to have been in the top three students in her year. I was proud to see her finishing her schooling. She had studied hard and dedicated herself to her studies and to helping her mother care for her father. After taking photographs of her in her cap and gown, I presented her with a Bible from her sponsor. I wished her all the best for her future and hoped she would find the words of life in the Bible to be a faithful guide. She had the talent and the determination to make something of herself.

When I took the time to look around me the evidence of appreciation was everywhere. Mayerli lived near to the health centre. She was just five years old, and every time I saw her she had the pink teddy bear she had received for Christmas from her sponsor under her arm.

Sonja came to visit me. I taught her how to sew patchwork cushion covers with an appliquéd flower design, while her children played with Tamara. She learnt quickly and set to work making them on the sewing machine we had given her. With the proceeds from her sewing she bought blocks and cement to improve her house. I also started to notice her children wearing clothes made by her from bright and bold fabrics. She kept fighting to provide the best she could for her children.

Hortencia made some jam from the guava fruit that was in season and brought it in for Monserrat and I to enjoy with her over a cup of herbal tea in the health centre. They were both enjoying their work and becoming ever more skilled in their tasks. They worked well together and went the extra mile to help patients who lived close by.

Rocio joined the sewing group. Bringing up her four children alone she struggled to make ends meet and had asked me a long while before if she could sell me some of her goods. The sales of items in the UK had been good enough that year to be able to give her some work now, and she was very keen to start. I asked her to make some dinosaur pencil cases out of felt in bold orange and green. She set to work straightaway.

I chuckled to myself as the gas lorry made its way along the road. "Housewives, housewives come and buy your gas cylinder so you can cook for your family", they called over the loud speaker as they passed by. Their turn of phrase tickled me with its machismo assumptions. I no longer took offense.

A visitor arrived from Britain who was sponsoring a lad in Julio Moreno through secondary school. I had the great privilege of taking Clive to meet Juan.

Juan lived in a tiny house on stilts made of roughly cobbled together wooden planks. The divisions in the house to create a bedroom were made of plastic sheeting. Juan and his mother invited us in warmly, delighted to be able to meet this generous man who was helping them from across the ocean. I acted as interpreter as they talked about his faith, his school, his favourite subjects and his love of football. Clive showed them photos of his family, including his baby granddaughter. We struggled to do justice to the food they had prepared for us.

It was a special meeting of two such different people, linked by a simple act of kindness. Clive went away touched by his visit, their poverty and their warm welcome. I enjoyed being able to introduce Clive to the lad he was helping. It brought to life the reality that was so hard to express with paper and words. Reaching out and touching lives in person made an indelible impression. Clive went away and found more sponsors for more children. What an endorsement of the work. I felt encouraged and spurred on to achieve even more for God.

I felt more at home with Vladimir's family too. Vladimir's mother went to harvest some maize that had grown on the flower farm. She, along with Vladimir's sister and Granny set about grinding up the maize and mixing it together with cheese to make humitas. The mixture was wrapped in banana leaves and steamed until it became a cake-like texture. We were all invited to enjoy them with hot sweet coffee. The coffee making was a ritual brought by Great-Granny from Colombia. She stood by the huge saucepan straining the sweet coffee through a sieve with a ladle, as Vladimir's Mum served the humitas. The whole family was chatting and laughing over the most recent antics of the cousins who were visiting. Tamara played happily with her Grandfather, their laughter the perfect accompaniment to our feast.

The conversation turned to cooking and the restaurants the women present had worked in in their time. They told of the tradition of stirring the soup with a human femur bone as it was thought to bring luck in the form of customers flocking to the door. My mind boggled as to where they had obtained the bones.

I shared that I had once heard of a restaurant in Santo Domingo being closed because they had been serving human flesh. Some friends had been frequent customers there and were horrified to think what they may have been inadvertently eating.

Everyone laughed and agreed it could only have been that they were using a bone to stir the soup. General opinion was that it was only the Chinese restaurants that put weird and wonderful meats in their special fried rice, such as snake, dog and rat. Vladimir claimed he had heard of a factory near by making sausages from horse meat. No one believed him.

I privately resolved to stick to eating what was identifiable as I appreciated deeply being part of this remarkable family. The Bible promises to put the lonely in families, and that was what He had done for me.

## CHAPTER TWENTY-SIX

# Happy Birthday

Vladimir, Tamara and I all went up to Quito to meet my Mum off the plane. I was so excited she was finally coming to visit us. I had lots to show her and so many people for her to meet. She was my number one supporter and I was excited she would finally understand what I was trying to do.

It was a good morning for travelling the spectacular decent through the Andes Mountains to Santo Domingo. The usual mist had lifted and Mum had a wonderful view of the immense mountain peaks and yawning valleys that dropped away from the road alarmingly. Everything was green, and there were many waterfalls to be spotted on route, cascading down the steep mountainsides. There were hairpin bends to navigate and the remains of landslides caused by the heavy rains to skirt around. We saw a vehicle left on the side of the road after a recent crash, and drove slowly to avoid plummeting to the depths visible below us.

Once we arrived back in hot sweaty Santo Domingo we made Mum comfortable in our second bedroom, and showed her round the village. Mum coped very well with the heat. She walked around without tiring or complaining. She was far too occupied taking in all the new sights, sounds and smells to notice any discomfort.

She loved spotting the many birds that visited our garden, coming to feast on the bananas we kept outside. There were birds of every colour, size and description. There were shiny jet black birds with a bright yellow stripe, beautiful blue, yellow and green parrot-like birds, light brown birds with very fine features, and huge birds of prey to be seen circling high above us. Added to that were the whirring, fast hummingbirds that hovered and darted amongst the flowers.

There were many plants in our garden that Mum also had growing in her conservatory at home. There were the variegated leaves that grew in reds, greens and whites in great profusion. They grew so much larger in the great outdoors of Santo Domingo than they grew indoors as pot plants in Scotland. There were orchids and heart shaped anthuriums, as well as brown-eyed-susans and busy-lizzies growing as weeds everywhere you looked.

Tamara also loved to be in the garden and to pick the flowers. She and Mum wandered outside together becoming reacquainted, while I prepared the lunch. It was beautiful to watch them together. I was so happy they had this chance to spend time together.

In the afternoon we took a trip to a nearby swimming pool with the health promoters, so that my Mum could meet them. We all piled into the pick-up truck and drove along in the sun to the pool, children in tow. Everyone had a good time splashing about in the warm water in the fresh air. I acted as translator for Mum so she could chat to the ladies. Hortencia told her about the chickens she was rearing for the eggs she could sell, Mery told her about her daughter who was doing well at secondary school, and Monserrat introduced her to her daughter Sayuri, who was having a good go at swimming, and losing some of her shyness at last.

Mum came along with me to the health centre some mornings that week to help with Tamara and to see the kind of patients that came along. She met Don Sofonias, more poorly again after having suffered another stroke, and another elderly man concerned he had been struck by lightning the night before.

Rocio, whose baby I had delivered, came in with her little boy, who had an abscess needing to be lanced. We tried to do it as gently as possible, but it was still very painful for the poor wee mite. At least once it was done the horrible pain he had been suffering before was in large part relieved. I kept a stash of prizes for children who came in and he was well rewarded for his bravery.

Suddenly there was a commotion outside and a ten year old girl was brought in crying loudly. She had been bitten by a neighbour's dog on her face and was in shock as much as anything. We cleaned up her wounds and made sure she had a tetanus injection, and sent her away with antibiotics. For once the neighbour acted responsibly, paying for the girl's treatment and shooting the dog in question.

Next we saw a Mum with her eight month old baby who had a cold. After checking him over and recommending some remedies to help control his fever and congestion, his Mum asked, "Doctor is it alright to give him watermelon to eat? My Granny and Aunt say that I should not give it to him as he has a cold. They say it will make him cough." I reassured her it was good to give him fruit and vegetables to eat, and that watermelon was full of vitamins that would help him get better, not make him worse. Feeling brave now she also asked if she could bath her baby. She said she had not done so for two days, as he had the cold and she was afraid she would make him worse, but she had noticed he was starting to get some red spots on his skin. I also reassured her that she should indeed bath her baby and keep him clean to prevent pneumonia. She looked convinced by my arguments in favour of bathing, and said she was away to give him a good clean.

Mum and I took a wander around the houses near to the health centre and I introduced her to an elderly couple, the Solartes. He had suffered a stroke, and had been left with weakness down the left side of his body. He found it difficult to work in the fields swinging a machete about at his age. His wife had a club foot which had never been treated, so she walked with a pronounced limp, on the side of her damaged foot instead of the sole.

They lived in a shelter (you could hardly call it a house), made with split bamboo walls, and plastic and rusty zinc roofing. The house was built on stilts which looked like they would collapse at any moment. The floor sloped and some of the wooden planks making the floor were now rotten and breaking. You had to be very careful where you stepped or you would fall through the floor altogether. The walls had gaps in them too, and the mosquitos and other wildlife entered at will.

The couple had lived there for four years by then, and really the materials they had used had reached the end of their lifespan, now succumbing to the effects of the humidity, torrential rain and wood worm. It was obvious that they needed a new home, but they had no resources to build one with. Their daughters' homes were in pretty much the same state and they were not in a position to help their parents.

The Solartes had come from Colombia many years before, and as they were not Ecuadorean citizens were not entitled to any government help with housing or benefits. They relied heavily on the generosity of their neighbours, and each weekend took a trip to town to beg the rejects from the fruit and vegetables in the market. They would fill up a sack with these damaged vegetables, and load it onto the back of the open air bus to take home to eat during the week. I had been told on good authority that on occasion the wily couple managed to off load someone else's sack of good quality produce, instead of their own, in order to enjoy better fare from time to time.

My Mum took their plight to heart and determined to try and raise the funds to enable them to have a new house. She took some photos of their current dwelling, and of them, ready to show folk back home. She was touched by meeting people living in such dire conditions, and wanted to do what she could to help them.

Tamara's first birthday dawned and we had decided to have a party which was a kind of compromise between Ecuadorean and British traditions.

The day started with present giving, opening the gifts sent by her British Aunts and Uncles and of course her Granny. Her Ecuadorean Grandparents then took Tamara into town to buy her a present.

Mum and I took advantage of Tamara's absence to get cracking with preparing the food for the party. We made little sandwiches, topped crackers, prepared salad and pop-corn, and baked some cookies and cakes. The birthday cake was a homemade chocolate cake iced to look like a little girl.

We had invited Tamara's numerous second cousins, her playmates and the health promoter's daughters. Everyone arrived somewhat late, the last stragglers arriving about an hour after the time given to them on the invitation in true Ecuadorian style.

We started with some games. First up was the British classic pass-the-parcel, which was enjoyed greatly as much as anything for the novelty factor. Next we played pin the tail on the donkey, followed by some simple running races before we moved on to the food and cake.

Finally we produced the piñata that Vladimir had bought for the party. It was a pink princess with a frilly skirt, filled with whistles, party poppers, plastic bracelets, sweets and confetti.

Vladimir lifted Tamara up in her beautiful party dress, and helped her to pull open the base of the piñata. The children fell upon the stash below and grabbed all the booty they could, stuffing it into their skirts and pockets. They were all very happy with their sweets and trinkets.

I also made up little party bags for Mum to take back to my siblings, which included a photo of Tamara in her party dress on her special day. We had all thoroughly enjoyed Tamara's birthday. I was so glad my Mum had been able to share in the special day. It made the world seem a smaller place, the distances that separated us less significant.

Living amongst children who had so very few toys, I felt Tamara was very privileged in being given so many beautiful, good quality toys and books by so many members of our family and friends. Sometimes Vladimir and I reflected that it seemed some children came into this world with absolutely no one to love and worry about them, while others were surrounded by those who loved and cared for them. There seemed such a huge chasm between the two, yet the children lived next door to each other and played together. I hoped Tamara would grow up grateful for all she was privileged to receive, not take it for granted.

## CHAPTER TWENTY-SEVEN

# A Stitch in Time

One of the things I had most looked forward to doing with my Mum was introducing her to the sewing group she did so much for as she sold their goods for them voluntarily in the UK.

I had asked the group to come along to our house Monday afternoon to check over the goods Mum was going to take back with her for them, and of course so that they could meet Mum.

The ladies arrived on mass at our gate, along with their respective children, actually on time for once. They were nervous at meeting the visitor and rather shyly came in and gave the usual kisses all around.

I seated them on the plastic stools I kept on the patio, under the thatched roof shelter, so that they were shaded from the sun. A small breeze wove its way delightfully across the patio, welcomed by all as they were hot from their walk to my house.

I introduced my Mum and tried to explain the hard work she did for them, entirely voluntarily, as she sold their goods in churches and sales in the UK whenever she was given the opportunity. I am not sure if they really understood or not, but they were certainly pleased to meet her.

Mum had brought some little gifts for them and their children; some hair slides and soaps, notebooks and colouring pencils, postcards of Scotland and laminated pictures from calendars. This broke the ice. The children were excitedly putting the pretty hair ornaments in their hair, and drawing with the pencils, chattering away as they did so. The ladies were fascinated by the pictures, examining the photos of Highland cattle and seals with exclamations of wonder. Their experience of the world did not extend far beyond Santo Domingo – perhaps Quito and the beach on rare occasions.

I handed out the goods that needed corrections made to them, and the ladies all set to work with their needles. We had been making fabric painted peg bags, aprons for adults and children, toiletry bags and jewellery rolls. Some needed a popper fastening centralised, a piece of embroidery tidied up, or loose thread ends removed.

While the ladies stitched and snipped Mum chatted to them, finding out more about their stories and how they were getting on.

Aida and her cousins with whom I had started the sewing project were all present. Karla was in her final year at secondary school, and very excited to be finishing. She talked about her plans to look for a job when she graduated from school in accounting, so that she could attend university in the evenings. She wanted to study business administration. Angela was in her third year of secondary school and had to choose which subjects she wished to specialise in for the next year. She was thinking of chemistry and physics. Her ambition was to study to be a doctor. Mishel had a sponsor helping her as she started out in secondary school. Her ambition was to be a lawyer to defend the poor.

It was wonderful to see their bright faces, full of dreams and ambitions, shining with the hope that these goals would actually become reality. They were fighting against many odds, but I shared their aspirations and believed they really could make them come true. They had certainly stuck with the sewing faithfully week after week for several years now, and very much appreciated the help that the extra income was to them.

Tania, the young lady allowed to study because her parents feared she would never marry, was also in her third year now, and was also faithfully making the most of her studies. She obtained good grades in all her classes and was choosing accountancy as her specialty for the next year, with the hope of a book keeping job when she finished school. I did not share her parent's fear that she would never marry. She was a beautiful lass, with her hair in tight ringlets framing her high cheek bones and beautiful dark eyes. I was sure she would have plenty of offers, and only hoped she did indeed wait long enough to finish her schooling first.

Jenny was doing an amazing job producing her bead jewellery. She sat polishing them, making sure there was no rust on the fixings, as sometimes occurred due to the humidity. She showed my Mum the sets she had made with matching earrings, bracelets and necklaces. All her designs were her own, and she came up with hundreds of different ideas, including fine crochet, zigzag effects and cascades of beads. Her use of colour was very appealing, and she cleverly included ribbons, chain, and bead weaving in her work.

She too was in her third year, and was sticking to her ambition to be a teacher. My Mum had been a teacher, so the two of them chatted a little about life in a Primary school, as Mum encouraged her to keep following her dreams. Jenny was a very patient person, gentle and methodical in manner, and good with young children. I was sure she would be a very good teacher and hoped she would achieve her dream.

Señora Maria was sitting with her hoard of children running about the place. I told Mum how pleased I was that all the children were now attending school, thanks to sponsors, and looked set to pass the year this time. Jacquelina was due to finish primary school this year, and was very, very proud to be the first in her family to do so. She was now sixteen years old. Araceli was holding her own at school, despite her blind eye. Her whole manner was changing, as she found self-confidence with her new successes. Kassandra, John and Gabriela were also doing well, and grateful for all the help they received. They called me "Auntie".

I pointed out to Mum that Gabriela was cuddling the doll she had received as her present at the Christmas party. She was rarely seen without it. It was lovely to see her gift was so appreciated. Mum snapped a beautiful photo of the unassuming little girl.

I showed Mum the number books Señora Maria had stitched in felt. It had been quite a feat to help her to make these with all the numbers in the right order and the right way up! As Señora Maria did her final correction, her face broke out into a wide beam. She exclaimed with great enthusiasm how happy she was that she had learnt to sew, and that although at times it was difficult for her to make certain items, she felt so extremely pleased when she finally managed it. As she flicked through a book with Mum you could just see how absolutely proud she was of the finished product. I shared a smile with Mum. Despite the frustrations sometimes I had a soft spot for Señora Maria and I did hope we would be able to guide and help her children to a better future.

Señora Fredis, whose wedding I had been to, was also present with her children Diana, Edwin and Milena. Milena was now running around the place chattering nineteen to the dozen, quite the little girl, no longer a baby. Diana, now a teenager, helped her Mum do much of the sewing work. She was gradually taking over as she developed confidence and ability. Between them they did very careful work. Diana had learnt to use the sewing machine, and ran up some great bags and very cute rag dolls. She made some like the Colorado Indians of Santo Domingo which sold very well with their bright colours and attention to detail. Fredis was a talented embroiderer, who did many of the embellishments and finishing touches. They made a great team.

Diana was also in her third year of secondary school, and doing well in her studies. She often turned up with her English homework, hoping she would be able to quiz me and get some help with it.

New to the group was Martha. Martha was deaf and dumb, a single mother to two delightful little girls. They used their own version of sign language between them to communicate, and her daughters managed to explain to Martha what I wanted her to make with surprising ease.

Martha had had a sewing machine for many years. She was a real whizz with her machine and made her daughters beautiful dresses and skirts. I was pleased to be able to put some work her way, and gave her the task of making some patchwork bags from a sack of scraps of material we had been donated. She did not disappoint me and made many beautiful bags. Her work had a real professional finish to it. I showed them to Mum who was very pleased with the touch of elegance and class.

We decided to have a photo shoot and asked the women and girls to model the bags, jewellery and other items they had made. We had a fun half hour, filled with giggles and laughter as the girls got into the spirit of the exercise and modelled with elegance and style.

We used the photos later to make a catalogue of the items for sale, to be sent to friends and supporters. Having those who had made the items starring in the photos gave it a very authentic feel.

As the time came for the ladies to depart Aida's family produced a beautiful flower arrangement they had brought for my Mum as a thank you. They used the English they had to thank her very prettily for all her hard work for them, and brought tears to our eyes. It was so unexpected. It really touched me to see their appreciation; that they did not take this help they received for granted. It made a fitting end to a heart-warming afternoon.

Mum returned to Scotland with the people she had met in her heart. She dedicated herself to selling the crafts with new purpose, as she was now doing it for women and children she had met, touched and loved. She sent photos of the children to their sponsors with little anecdotes of how they were progressing, and she did not forget the Solarte couple, living under plastic.

## CHAPTER TWENTY-EIGHT

# House Raising

It was a season of house building in the villages. The new government was investing money in helping the poorest families with their own simple block house. Of course there were certain requisites that applicants had to fulfil. The first was that they had to have a plot of land with title deeds in their own name. They also had to be Ecuadorean nationals, and qualify to receive benefits. This included the poorest with young children, disabled people, and elderly people. They also needed a certain amount of initiative, persistence and patience to be able to collect together the required papers, present them on time and then keep going to the housing office to enquire about progress on their application.

A group of twenty applicants was accepted in our area to have a house built. It included some very appropriate families, such as Aida's, Jeovhanny's and deaf Martha's. To have a safe, waterproof block house was an enormous benefit to them.

Others could not apply or else had their applications rejected. Don Sofonias could not apply because he was

Colombian. Araceli's family could not apply because they did not have papers for their land nor the money to get them, and the Solarte couple could not apply because they were Colombian.

My Mum was doing a great job talking to everyone she met about the needs she had seen in Ecuador, and in particular the Solarte couple who needed a house. She gave talks in churches, and showed family and friends her photos, and within a few months had raised the money that we needed to be able to build them a block house.

Vladimir was very excited we could help this old couple in this way. He asked his good friend Darwin to be the builder for the house. They went to mark out the dimensions for the laying of the foundations to begin. The house was to have two bedrooms and a kitchen/living area. The couple were overjoyed at the prospect of a new house, and came to investigate what was going on. When they heard there were to be two bedrooms they suggested four might be a better idea, so they could receive guests – including visitors from the UK who they imagined might come to see the house they had so kindly paid for. Vladimir came home chuckling about it. The old folk made the craziest suggestions sometimes. Maybe they were just so proud of the prospect of a proper house they were imagining showing it off in all its splendour.

Their old house collapsed of its own accord, finally succumbing to humidity and rotting away. All that remained was a pile of soggy bamboo. The ground was cleared ready for the foundations to be laid.

Vladimir took some of the local lads to the river with him to collect large stones to put in the foundations. A neighbour lent his lorry to go and collect the blocks from the block maker, and more volunteers went along to help load and unload the thousand blocks. It was good to see how people were willing to help.

Work began on the foundations, and I wandered down to see their progress one afternoon. The cement mixer was whirring as the workmen tipped the sand and cement into it. It was surprising to see how quickly the construction was taking shape, with the concrete floor being laid already.

Next the blocks were laid, building up the outside walls and then the divisions inside to form the bedrooms. Darwin was very careful laying the blocks, placing them evenly to make the house strong and attractive looking. Some spectators heckled asking why bother making the house look so nice when it was just a work of charity. Darwin did not share this attitude and always made sure he did a good job no matter who it was for.

Once the walls were completed the wooden beams were secured on top ready for supporting the roof.

Vladimir went and bought the zinc sheets for the roof. They were fixed in place and the house looked great. The front door was secured into place next. Then Vladimir measured up the windows, and found some that fitted perfectly in a recycle yard. They had swirly black iron grates that gave real style to the house.

Darwin finished the kitchen by making a cement kitchen bench with tiles on top of the work surface and up the wall, and a kitchen sink. He also made a shelf under the kitchen bench for their pots and pans. Just like that the house was ready for occupation.

The Solartes moved in their worldly goods very quickly. They only possessed a bed, a couple of hard chairs, plates, spoons, pans and a four ring cooker top. Their clothes were kept in cardboard boxes. They were delighted with their new abode. We took lots of photos of them, and sent them to my Mum to share with those who had so generously donated the funds for the house. Darwin, Vladimir and I shook hands in celebration at this achievement; an elderly couple able to live out their years in safety and comfort. We were all so glad to have been able to help them.

It was good to be able to sleep easy that night, while the rain battered the roof of our house knowing that the elderly and vulnerable couple were safely out of the rain and would be sleeping peacefully too.

More fundraising was inspired by this story relayed back to supporters in the UK, with photos of the couple enjoying their new house. This time it took the form of marathon running, sponsored mountain climbing and bicycle riding.

We decided to use these funds to build a house for an old man who had been left with crippled hands due to untreated arthritis, Daniel Paz. He still worked in the fields, but could not grip his machete very well. He usually stayed with whoever he was working for at the time, but did own a plot of land. His brother and his wife were living there in a plastic tent-like shelter. His sister-in-law had advanced Parkinson Disease, and could barely walk unaided. They had no toilet and had to find a spot in the garden to do their necessaries. They were all Colombians and did not qualify for any government help.

Vladimir, Tamara and I were at the beach, relaxing before starting the building of the next house, when Vladimir received a shocking phone call. Darwin had been killed outright in a motorbike accident. The whole village was stunned and grief stricken.

There were motorbike accidents along our road seemingly every Sunday. Sometimes due to alcohol, sometimes speed and the sheer volume of traffic on a sunny day when many people from the city came for a day out to the rivers. Darwin himself had been a patient of ours some three times for minor injuries sustained by coming off his bike. However this time it seemed to have been a freak accident.

Darwin had been driving his bike, with a friend on the back, up near one of the most popular bathing spots, when a tall tree had fallen straight on top of him. Death had been instantaneous. His friend escaped without a mark. Everyone was shocked that this popular, hard-working young man was suddenly gone.

It was of course especially hard on his family. He was the only son, the youngest child with three older sisters. He had still lived with his parents, and had done all he could to help them. They were devastated. The whole village turned out to the wake to accompany them through the two nights that followed.

Darwin's body was placed in a coffin and was on view in the doorway to his house. A white tent was erected, to cover the many chairs that were lined up underneath. These chairs were filled by the neighbours coming to pay their respects and accompany the family in this time of grief.

I gave Darwin's elderly parents, both regular patients of mine, heartfelt hugs. His mother always made me feel like I was in the presence of royalty; she was such a dignified woman. It cut me to the core to see her terrible grief for her only son.

Darwin's sister Christina was a hard working woman always volunteering to do things for the community. Vladimir helped her selling flowers she grew in Quito each week. She quietly came and served us a drink her head bowed by the weight of her grief at losing such a dearly loved little brother.

Vladimir stayed all night, accompanying the family and his now departed good friend Darwin.

They decided to have the wake for two nights, not just one, to give family members time to arrive from Colombia. As soon as Darwin's Aunt arrived it was time for the funeral.

This took place in the village Catholic Church. The priest held the mass, while the attenders were crowded out of the door. I was asked by Darwin's sisters to accompany their mother in the funeral car outside. They were worried about how the devastating loss was affecting her, but she had refused to stay at home during the funeral.

It was heart breaking to see the deep sorrow evident at the loss of such a dear son, brother and friend. There was great solidarity in how so many people gathered round to support those most affected by this tragedy.

After the service, Darwin's body was taken to the local cemetery. More words were spoken by the priest and many people went to have a last look at Darwin's face. Even small children were held up to say their last good-bye. "Did you go and say good bye to your Uncle?" Darwin's mother asked her eight year old granddaughter. It was very important to her that she had.

Darwin's body was laid to rest in a cement tomb above the ground, and flowers were laid at its entrance. He would be sorely missed.

That evening, back home after the funeral, Vladimir and I remembered all the things we had appreciated most about Darwin. He had been a lifelong friend to Vladimir and had worked with us with such good will on the toilets and house building projects. "You never know what tomorrow will bring, do you?" Vladimir remarked. "We can be here one moment and gone the next. May we make the most of each day God grants us, live our lives to the full."

"We should pray for Darwin's family too." I replied with great sadness in my heart. "They are going to miss him very much. A parent never imagines their child dying before them. They are going to need God's comfort in the days ahead."

I think God worked a little miracle for that dear family in the days that followed. Darwin's sister Christina discovered she was expecting a baby, seventeen years after giving birth to her first daughter. She and her husband had given up hope of another child. Darwin's memory would of course never fade, but Christina's blossoming pregnancy became a source of hope and healing for the whole family. They began to focus on the precious gift of this totally unexpected but deeply desired new life on its way.

Vladimir had to look for a new builder to take on the building of the house for Daniel Paz. Once again he set to work organising the materials required to build with, and supervised the workers. The house took shape quickly, and the three elderly people took refuge in their new home, very grateful for what seemed to them a palace in comparison to the conditions they had been living in before.

The tragedy reminded us how short and fragile life is. We are like flowers in the garden, here today and gone tomorrow. Yet we were determined to keep on living our lives in a manner worthy of the wonderful love of God; to show His love to those around us one person at a time while God granted us life and breath.

## CHAPTER TWENTY-NINE

# Twists and Turns

As the days went by Vladimir and I found our equilibrium, created our own mini-culture within our home, shaped our own way of caring for and bringing up our precious daughter. We learned to give and take, to mix and match, and found we could enjoy the infinite variety God has created in this world of ours.

I woke each day to thank God for His many blessings to me and most especially for granting me that most amazing gift of a family that loves me. Every time Tamara looked up and ran to greet me crying, "Mummy, Mummy" with a huge smile on her face, joy flooded my heart. Every time Vladimir caught Tamara and I into a big bear hug and told us that he loved us, happiness invaded my soul.

I learned to cope with successes and failures, to do all I could and then to leave God's precious children in His hands. When I was hurt and broken, I learned to go straight to Him for healing. And as I watched God work His miracles in people's lives I made friends along the way.

My heart sank as a local village man, Don Lucho, came in to tell us that he had stepped on a dirty nail a few days previously. He was a regular client of ours with diabetes. We had helped him to heal up a small ulcer on his toe a year previously and had come to appreciate this hard working family man who had raised not only his own children but also several of his grandchildren.

The foot was badly infected, red, swollen and full of pus. This time the problem was much more serious. I had to send him to the hospital for intravenous antibiotics and they opened up his foot and removed the dead material. His big toe developed gangrene. The bone was exposed and black. He went home for the weekend and was supposed to go back to the hospital to have part of his foot amputated on the Monday. Instead he came to us, hoping against hope that we would be able to save his foot.

I was not optimistic. His toe did not look good. He did not look good. He was gaunt and sickly looking. However Don Lucho was adamant he wanted to at least try dressings for a few days to see if there would be any improvement.

So praying to our Heavenly Father for this dear man, we washed his toe and I cut away the gangrene. He had no feeling in his toe, so did not require anaesthesia. We dressed it with honey, and told him to come back the next day. I could not sleep that night fearing what we might find in the morning. The next morning the toe was much the same. I was relieved it was not any worse.

Anxiously we watched his toe day by day, worrying more gangrene would develop. But it never did. After a couple of weeks there was a marked improvement. The feeling started returning to his toe. He was delighted to be able to feel pain again. He himself looked much better. Colour returned to his face and his eyes regained their sparkle.

I treated his diabetes aggressively, continued daily dressings and we all prayed fervently for his foot. Gradually, almost unperceptively, beautiful red healthy flesh began to form, filling the hole and enveloping the bone. The human body's capacity to heal itself never ceased to amaze me. We were bystanders watching God work a little miracle for Don Lucho.

Once the crater in his foot had all filled in the skin began to form, creeping in around the edges, gaining ground and taking new terrain slowly but surely.

Don Lucho's family stood amazed that their father was well again, able to work in the fields and walk for miles. I was so thankful he was indeed completely better against all odds. He was one very happy and relieved man. The day I discharged him he gave me a heart-felt hug and a kiss. The tears in his eyes betrayed his emotion at having a healthy foot restored instead of a dreaded amputation.

I shared his jubilation, and was so happy I had been God's hands for that man. Along the way I had made a friend.

It could only have been a couple of weeks later that he asked me to visit his grandson. Andres was a sixteen year old lad who had been battling cancer for four years by then. I shall never forget that visit. It is etched in my memory forever.

Andres was skeletally thin, lying groaning on his bed, vomiting relentlessly. He was so young. He should have been out playing the football he loved with his mates. He should have been full of ambition and pursuing the girls. My heart broke at the sight of him.

"Doctorita, please help me," he pleaded earnestly, desperation in his voice. "I cannot stand this anymore. I should have made the most of life. I should have lived life to the full while I had the chance. I so regret not doing so."

Kneeling by his bed I grasped his hand as his parents slipped out of the room to allow us to talk. He gripped my hand like a man who is drowning. "Please can you give me something to end this," he pleaded, "I do not want to go on like this."

I looked at him with great compassion and searched for words to say, "You know I cannot do what you ask me Andres, but I can help you. I will give you these injections for the pain and vomiting, so that you can rest. You will feel better if you can rest. Our lives are in God's hands. He has his time for you and your family. They want to have every possible moment with you."

He died later that night. I could not go to his funeral. I did not want to see his suffering face again. It was already etched in my memory, full of regrets and pain. Instead I knelt and took the pain to Jesus. I took his family to Jesus in prayer. I took his younger brother and sister to Jesus. I took Don Lucho to Jesus. I took my questions to Jesus, about why He had allowed Andres to suffer so, and left them in his nail-marked hands. I allowed the Holy Spirit to touch my wounds, and I prayed with all my heart that I would have the chance to help others who were dying much more than I had been able to help Andres.

Don Lucho did not come for a few weeks. He was too upset, too devastated by the loss of his grandson.

And then one morning he came for a check-up, as life and hope called him forwards and onwards once again. He called me "Andreita", counting me a dear friend, and I was privileged to think of him likewise. I learned from his strength, his determination to move forward into the future. The blows and tragedies we received in life were not reasons to give up. The unanswered questions and mysteries were not reasons to stop trying. It was time to open our hearts to the next needy person on our doorstop.

Christina was nearing the end of her miracle pregnancy. Her husband was so delighted they were going to have another baby. Her seventeen year old daughter could not wait to meet her sibling. Her bereaved parents were waiting with open hearts to hold their tiny granddaughter. But Christina was sick. She needed to be in hospital. They did not have the money to keep her in for many nights.

I think hundreds of people must have prayed for Christina and the baby. It all seemed such a gift from God, this miracle baby coming after Darwin's tragic death. It could not end in disaster as well. It simply could not.

Once Christina self-discharged from the hospital I visited her at home, monitoring her closely, alert in case her condition worsened, counselling her family on how best to care for her, giving her the medicines she needed.

Christina kept on going, until finally, at last, the obstetrician decided it was time to deliver her baby. Rafaela was born absolutely tiny, but she was a fighter and rapidly started to gain weight. Christina was unwell for several weeks, but then also regained her strength and health. Many hearts were made glad by this precious new life, this symbol of hope and of God's mercy. I held Rafaela in my arms, still only a few days old, as I sat on Christina's bed at home. She felt as light as a feather. Her little face was beautiful and baby smooth. She slept as if there were no troubles in the world, perfectly trusting of her mother to care for her. She reminded me that this was how I should be with my Heavenly Father, not worried and anxious, but full of faith in Him.

I felt so privileged to be able to share these life-defining moments with people in the village. I wondered at how far I had come since my arrival in the orphanage all those years before. I wondered at the affection I felt for these people, the love that must have been placed in my heart by God himself. I had come to Ecuador because a little boy had needlessly had his finger amputated, and now by God's grace I was saving limbs. I had come because a couple had tried to give me their baby, and now I was helping dearly loved babies be born safely to their parents. I could not imagine a better way to be spending the precious hours God granted me on this earth.

## CHAPTER THIRTY

# Iguana Eggs

And so I stay in Santo Domingo de los Tsachilas. I stay because there is still work to be done here. I stay because each day still brings new opportunities to serve a fellow human being. I stay because I never tire of watching the humming birds and because I love to see the orchids cascading from the trees in all their majestic elegance. I stay because my family and I are happy here.

Each new day is an adventure, an open page yet to be written. I never know whom I might meet or what new turn in the road there might be, but I know each day brings a new opportunity to make a difference in someone's life. What could be more exciting and fulfilling than that?

As I look around me, instead of seeing the mould, rot and decay, I open my eyes to the abundant tropical flowers, the rainbow coloured birds and the refreshing rains. They become symbols of renewal and hope, of new beginnings and the potential for growth.

I love to immerse myself in the rushing river, sheltered by the towering bamboo growing along the banks, sharing the water with the fish and the storks. I feel so free; free to be me, free to imagine and dream, free to make dreams come true for those around me.

Every now and then I make time to accompany Vladimir on the farm for a morning. We take our spades and set to work planting trees. We dig up the rich chocolate brown earth, and lovingly set in place fruit trees, hoping to still be around to harvest the fruit in five or ten years' time. We anticipate juicing the oranges, savouring the sweet lychees, milkshake making with the guanabanas and cake making with the cinnamon. We plant coconut palms, lemon and grapefruit trees, and harvest the already big avocado and cocoa bean trees.

Vladimir's love of this corner of the world, which produces so prolifically, emerald green in its fertility is infectious. He is so content carving a home for us on the farm. He is in his element looking after the plants and building a place of beauty for us all to enjoy. He has the opportunity to make his dreams a reality, to be creative, to provide and care for us.

I have the chance to continue to help those God places across my path, one at a time, to be His hands for them.

I stay for Jofre, a fourteen year old lad who dreams of being a motor mechanic, but whose parents did not send him to school last year because they could not afford the expense. How exciting to be able to give him the opportunity to attend school and pursue his dream, by finding him a sponsor.

I hope he will study hard and do the best he can. I hope he will end up with a job that pays him enough to look after his future family well, and lift them out of poverty. I hope he will be curious about this world in which we live and broaden his horizons. I hope he will take care of his parents in their old age, and pay forward the help he is receiving from us.

I stay for Jenny. She is fifteen years old and has not been able to start Secondary School because her Step-father spends his money on the three children that are his, and does not have enough left over to pay for Jenny as well. Jenny's face lit up as she shared her ambition of studying to be a book keeper. She confessed she loves mathematics. She is also a whizz kid on the football pitch.

I hope the sponsorship she receives will enable her to pursue her dream. I hope she will take the opportunity to study and put off having a family of her own until she finishes. I long for her to have the qualifications she needs to be able to work and support herself in the future. I hope she will acquire the knowledge she needs to discern truth from myth and to understand how to care for and educate her future children well. I hope she will receive the encouragement and love she needs, and that nothing will wipe the beautiful smile from her face. I hope she will understand deep in her soul that she has a Heavenly Father who loves her and cares for her.

I stay for patients like Maria. She is dying from terminal gastric cancer. There was sadly no way to cure her disease, but we can in some measure alleviate her suffering.

To get to her house we have to leave the car at the end of a path well into the countryside, and walk through green trees blossoming with flowers in a myriad of colours, as we listen to the birds chirping in the leafy branches. The path leads down to a stream, which has a tree trunk lain across it as a bridge. Afraid of falling in I sit down to shuffle myself across on my behind, not minding the comical sight that is to my companions.

As we walk up the hill to her house I take in the beautifully kept garden, the smartly painted walls and the immaculately clean house.

We find Maria lying in her bed. She was in pain when we first came, and vomiting all she attempted to ingest. We helped her husband buy some morphine patches for her. We were glad to have some funds to help towards the cost of them. When she has the patches in place Maria feels much more comfortable.

When she was still able to converse she shared about how she enjoyed watching television to pass away the time while her husband was out working in the fields. Her niece accompanied her and made sure she had all she needed.

This visit Maria is weaker and entering her final decline. She acknowledges us with a nod of her head and a squeeze of her hand, but is no longer able to speak. She is obviously in pain and her niece explains that they have not replaced her patch for lack of funds to buy more. We apply the last one, and make sure they have the necessary funds to go and buy more supplies. As the pain relief takes effect she visibly relaxes and sinks into a much needed sleep.

When the family first discovered Maria had cancer they took her all over the country desperately and frantically seeking a hospital or witchdoctor that could cure her. But the cancer was already too advanced.

Now there is a sense of acceptance in the house. The family know they have done all they could to help Maria, and are dedicated to caring for her until the end. They feel reassured that they have support during this distressing time in their life, and someone to ask for help.

We gratefully accept the lemon juice and bread that they offer us and chat to them as we eat and drink. When we leave Maria is sleeping peacefully with her son sitting by her side gently holding her hand.

I do not know how many days Maria has left in this world, but hope that her last days are peaceful ones, spent in the company of those she loves the most, and that her family will have good memories of their time together, not scarred by scenes of distressing pain and suffering.

I stay for the patients who regularly beat a path to the health centre seeking help for their complaints. Of course there are people all over the world with the same problems, but these are those I have the privilege of serving for now.

First today is a seventy year old woman who loves living on her small holding in the sticks, looking after her chickens and growing maize and manioc. She is recovering from a bout of acute pancreatitis, and her daughters are tearing their hair out because she refuses to rest, but wants to be out and about with her animals as usual. With a twinkle in her eyes she presents me with a live chicken in a sack "to make a good soup", and asks if I can give her some more of the pills that are helping her feel so much better.

I know Vladimir will be delighted to come home to a filling sancocho soup for tea: boiled up free range chicken with green banana thickening the broth, and fresh herbs and onion adding flavour. I thank her profusely, as she gratefully takes her fresh supply of medicines back with her to her outpost.

Next is a middle aged man with a leg wound. He had an accident a couple of months before and ended up with a macerated shin that was badly infected. After a gruelling few weeks of treatment with many injections of antibiotics and concoctions given intravenously at home, he had come to us feeling washed out and sick. By this time the infection was under control, so we had just given him tablets to take for a few more days and turned our attention to dressing the wound. Now it is almost healed. He is back at work and putting food on the table for his family. He is a happy man.

Señora Felicita is next. Her insulin, blood pressure medicines and asthma inhalers are being paid for by a church group in the UK who are sponsoring her. She gives me some fresh eggs from her chickens, and tells me her youngest son has now successfully finished his second year at High School. He is working during the holidays to save up for school next year, and so she apologises she has not had anyone to help her check her blood sugar for her. She cannot read the numbers, so they are meaningless to her. Her son normally notes them down for me to see.

She smiles her gratitude for the next month's supply of medication, and goes outside to wait for the bus back home. We have now been helping her with medications and check- ups for five years. It is good to see her looking so well and able to care for her family.

This afternoon I take Tamara to the river on the farm to swim with her friends in the water warmed by the hot sun. We see some iguana tracks and then spot their nests hosting their fragile eggs in the sand, and watch flocks of blue and green parrots weaving their way above us. The girls take their buckets and spades and make sand castles along the river's edge.

There are some watermelons growing in the sand. Tamara examines the biggest one to see if it is ready for eating yet. We cut it open and all enjoy munching on thick, sweet slices of the red fruit, the juice running down our chins.

Vladimir comes to join us once he finishes work, splashing into the river to cool off, romping and laughing with Tamara. Once everyone is tired out, we barbeque some green bananas with succulent pork ribs. When Tamara is tucked up in bed Vladimir and I relax in the hammock enjoying the coolness of the evening.

We chat about this new generation pursuing the education their parents never had. It is an exciting time to be living through; a time of opportunity and change. We wonder what will happen to these youngsters in the years ahead, what they will make of themselves, and what twists in the road the future holds for them. We chat about whom next to build a house for, who is most in need of a home.

We look to the challenge of educating our daughter, of her starting school, and wonder how best to manage her education. But beyond algebra and writing essays we hope she will learn to love God and her neighbour. We hope she will learn to be kind and generous. We hope she will appreciate living in this part of the beautiful world God has created. Most of all we hope she will know she is dearly loved.

As I listen to the now so familiar buzz of the insects, and feel the evening breeze caress my cheeks I silently give thanks for this place I call home. It is a privilege to feel useful, to be able to make a contribution in life. It is a place that still holds new dreams and hopes for me. It is where my imagination can run riot and my creativity can be expressed. It is a place where I have been blessed with love. It is a place that has brought me great joy. Being here continues to fill my heart with peace. I continue to feel it is the place God would have me be.

# Epilogue

Sometimes I look around me and all I see is huge need; so many children not going to school, so many children sick and suffering, so many deaths, accidents and tragedies. My mind and my heart cannot absorb it all. I cannot help them all. What I can do is so little, so miniscule on the scale of things.

But I can make a difference to some, to the next child that we find a sponsor for, to the next family we build a house for, to the next patient who comes with a leg ulcer dreading an amputation. I can make a difference to them. All of us can. All of us can help one more person who crosses our path.

And each person whose life we have the privilege to touch is a precious child of God. Even if we only have a glass of water to give them, Jesus said we are doing it for Him. So let's keep on doing it. Let's not forget. Let's not grow tired and weary. Let's continue to come to Him for the love and strength to keep on going, to keep on loving, to keep on helping.

I do not know what lies around the next bend in the road; I do not know what tomorrow will bring. I do not make plans far in advance anymore. We go from one day to the next, trusting God to meet our needs as we go.

But I do know that He is always with us. I can tell you that we are never in want. I can share with you that I am constantly surprised by His gifts of grace for me. And He has them for you too. I am so grateful He has blessed me with so much. But I know that the poor are always with us. While God grants me strength I will continue to serve them as best I know how. Join me in serving Him.

Andrea Gardiner was born in Kent and educated at Headcorn Primary School, Underhill Preparatory School, Ashford School for Girls and Edinburgh Medical School. She pursued training as a General Practitioner in Aberdeen and Shetland before heading to Ecuador in 2005. She is founder of the Christian Charity Project Ecuador, a ministry that reaches out through health care, child sponsorship, building projects and a sewing project. You can read her blog at www.andysintheandes.blogspot.com.

You can find out more about the charities mentioned in this book on the following websites;

Project Ecuador
www.projectecuador.co.uk

Orphaids working with those suffering from HIV in Ecuador and Colombia www.orphaids.org

Life in Abundance Trust working with the disabled in Ecuador www.liat-ecuador.org

Foundation Jersey working in palliative care in Ecuador www.fundacionjersey.org.je

Latin Link who send short and long term missionaries to many countries in South America www.latinlink.org.uk

Lightning Source UK Ltd.
Milton Keynes UK
UKOW041422121112

202080UK00001B/13/P